art/shop/eat
FLORENCE

Paul Blanchard

The City Centre

The Oltrarno

Santa Maria Novella

San Marco

Santa Croce

entertainment

planning

art glossary

maps

introduction

Situated on the banks of the Arno River and set among low hills covered with olive groves and vineyards, Florence is immediately captivating. Cradle of the Renaissance and home of Dante, Machiavelli, Michelangelo and the Medici, the city is almost overwhelming in its wealth of art, culture and history. Few other places can offer you the sheer number of monuments and museums you'll find here; nowhere is so much beauty concentrated in so small an area.

But Florence is much more than the sum of its museums. It is a living testimony to the intellectual prowess and aesthetic acumen of an age. It is also a reminder that individual and community interests are not contradictory, that, with sufficient commitments of financial and intellectual capital, self-interest and social responsibility can be reconciled; indeed, can work together to shape an ideal city.

As the capital of Tuscany, Florence is at the centre of one of Italy's richer agricultural regions. From the familiar Chianti to the inimitable Brunello di Montalcino and the lately famous Supertuscan wines, from tender Chianina beef to smooth pecorino cheese and delicate extra-virgin olive oil, the Tuscan table offers a wonderful combination of excellent fresh ingredients and simple, straightforward preparation, the cornerstones of Mediterranean cuisine.

And of course, people have been shopping in Florence for nearly a millennium: first for wool, then for artistic masterpieces and imaginative new financial products, and now for everything from *haute couture* to handcrafted crockery. Florence's million permanent residents and ten million annual visitors keep the shops thriving. The variety of wares they offer is astonishing; the level of quality, superb.

THE CITY
CENTRE

THE RELIGIOUS CENTRE

The Baptistery

OPEN	Mon-Sat 12.00-19.00, Sun 8.30-14.30
CLOSED	1/1, Easter, 8/9, 24/12, 25/12
CHARGES	€3; ticket sales end 30 minutes before closing
GUIDED VISITS	Audio tours available
WWW.	operaduomo.firenze.it
MAIN ENTRANCE	South door, Piazza San Giovanni

HIGHLIGHTS

Ghiberti's Gates of Paradise	Exterior
Architecture and decoration	Interior

Piazza San Giovanni and Piazza del Duomo take their names respectively from the baptistery and from the cathedral (*domus dei*, the 'house of God' in ecclesiastical Latin). Viewed as a whole, this open space and the buildings it holds form a monumental complex of great symbolic impact.

The oldest monument, and possibly the oldest piece of standing architecture in Florence, is the baptistery. To a Florentine of the 14c or 15c this handsome building offered unmistakable evidence of the city's Roman origins. The great minds of the Renaissance thought it had originally been a temple of Mars, erected to celebrate the Roman victory over Etruscan Fiesole. In reality it is the Romanesque reconstruction of a modest edifice of the 6c or 7c. Its octagonal form reflects Byzantine and Carolingian models – San Vitale in Ravenna, for instance, or Charlemagne's Palatine Chapel in Aachen.

EXTERIOR Outside, the building is entirely covered with white and green marble, set in simple geometric patterns that would serve as a model for much Florentine architecture of the following centuries.

Magnificent gilt bronze doors open on the baptistery's north, east and south sides. The **south door** is the oldest. Made in 1336 by sculptor Andrea Pisano, its main subjects are stories from the life of St John the Baptist. The beautiful surround was added in the 15c; the bronze statues (of *St John, Herod*, and *Salome*) on the wall above, in the 16c.

The **north door** was made in 1403-24 by Lorenzo Ghiberti, following a famous competition of 1401. The reliefs show New Testament stories, the Evangelists and the Church fathers. High up on the wall, 16c bronze statues represent *St John Praying*, a *Levite* and a *Pharisee*.

The **east door**, Ghiberti's most famous work and one of the great masterpieces of Renaissance sculpture, was executed between 1425 and 1452 with the help of numerous artists, including Michelozzo and Benozzo Gozzoli. Called by Michelangelo the **Gates of Paradise** because of their extraordinary beauty, its two gilt bronze panels are divided into ten squares (now replaced by copies; the originals are in the Museo dell'Opera), each of which is sculpted with virtuoso skill. The subjects are taken from the Old Testament. Reading from top to bottom, left to right, panels show stories of Adam and Eve, Cain and Abel, Noah, Abraham, Jacob and Esau, Joseph, Moses, Joshua, Saul and David, and Solomon.

INTERIOR Inside, the baptistery takes its cue from the great churches of Byzantium. The marble pavement is decorated with eastern Mediterranean geometric motifs. The ogival dome bears Byzantine-like **mosaics** by 13c and 14c Florentine and Venetian artists, one of whom may have been Cimabue. A huge *Last Judgement* occupies the three vault segments above the apse. In the main part of the ceiling, starting at the top, you can count six bands with representations of ornamental motifs, Christ and the Heavenly Host, stories from the Book of Genesis, stories of Joseph, stories of Christ and stories of St John.

To the right of the dais, between columns, is the *Tomb of antipope John XXIII* (Baldassare Coscia), who died in Florence in 1419. The tomb was designed by Michelozzo and bears an effigy by Donatello. The font, attributed to a follower of Andrea Pisano, was carved out of a single block of marble with low reliefs that represent eight scenes of baptism, one on each side, divided by pilasters decorated with floral motifs. It was probably commissioned to replace an earlier Romanesque font. Its iconographical intention is clearly to illustrate how the sacrament of baptism connects the faithful of today to an event that took place two thousand years ago but is renewed in every age.

The Cathedral

OPEN	**Cathedral**, Mon, Tues, Wed & Fri 10.00-17.00; Thur 10.00-15.30; Sat 10.00-16.45 (first Sat of the month 10.00-15.30); Sun 13.30-16.45 **Cupola**, Mon-Fri 8.30-19.00; Sat 8.30-17.40 (first Sat of the month 8.30-16.00) **Campanile**, daily 8.30-19.30
CLOSED	**Cathedral and Campanile**, 1/1, Easter, 15/8, 25/12 **Cupola**, Sun, 1/1, 6/1, Easter Thurs-Sun, 24/6, 15/8, 8/9, 1/11, Mon and Tues of the first week of Advent, 25/12, 26/12
CHARGES	**Cathedral**, free; **Campanile** and **Cupola**, €6; ticket sales end 40 minutes before closing
TELEPHONE	**055 230 2885**
WWW.	**operaduomo.firenze.it**
MAIN ENTRANCE	**Cattedrale di Santa Maria del Fiore**, left door of the façade

	Cupola, Porta dei Canonici (on the south side of the cathedral; 463 steps, no lift)
DISABLED ACCESS	**Cathedral**, Porta dei Canonici (south flank) (south flank)
GUIDED VISITS	Audio tours available
SERVICES	Bookshops at the **Cathedral** and **Campanile**

HIGHLIGHTS

Architecture and decoration   Interior

Cupola, the climb to the top

The cathedral of Florence is dedicated to the Virgin of the Annunciation, called Santa Maria del Fiore from the white lily which Gabriel, in traditional iconography, presents to the young Mary as a symbol of her immaculate conception. The church stands on the site of the old cathedral of Santa Reparata, founded in the early Christian period and rebuilt several times. In the 13c this building was deemed too small and humble for the proud new Florentine republic, and a new design was commissioned from the skilled architect and follower of Giotto, Arnolfo di Cambio. The ambitious new building was begun in 1296 and took almost 150 years to complete.

THE CHURCH

Arnolfo died soon after ground was broken, and the direction of works passed to other architects, notably **Francesco Talenti** and **Andrea Orcagna**, who added much to the original design. By 1417 the building was substantially finished; all that remained to be built was the dome. This was to be the largest dome of its time and the most complex engineering project since antiquity. Its construction posed serious technical problems.

In 1418 Filippo Brunelleschi and Lorenzo Ghiberti jointly won the public competition for its construction; shortly afterwards **Brunelleschi** took over. After careful study of the works of

Duomo, Baptistery and Campanile

antiquity, enhanced by some very original thinking, he proposed an astonishing solution: a gridlike 'skeleton' made up of 24 vertical ribs reinforced by horizontal elements. Without utilizing a fixed wood framework, only mobile scaffolding, he had his masons lay the bricks in a herringbone pattern forming concentric bands or rings that diminish in diameter as the structure gets higher. In this way he was able to create a structural system capable of carrying its own weight (estimated around 37,000 metric tonnes) in every phase of its construction. But Brunelleschi's most innovative engineering feat was the making of a second dome whose purpose was to share the structure's downward and outward thrust. The dome, without the lantern (a small octagonal temple with buttresses that was designed by Brunelleschi, but made by sculptor **Andrea Verrocchio** a few years later), was completed in 1436. It was immediately recognized as a major architectural achievement.

EXTERIOR The outside of the cathedral is a masterful blend of local marbles: white from Carrara, green from Prato, and red from southern Tuscany. Its design, though complex, effortlessly joins Romanesque, Gothic and Renaissance stylistic motifs in a composition of singular grace and harmony. The façade was built in the 19c in a Gothic Revival style to replace Arnolfo's uncompleted original, which was pulled down in the 16c.

CAMPANILE Giotto designed the graceful and unusual bell-tower next to the cathedral in 1334, but died before it was completed. His work was continued by Andrea Pisano and finished (in 1359) by Francesco Talenti. Rising dizzyingly over its modest square base, the tower is faced with the same coloured marbles as the duomo. The bas-reliefs and statues have been removed over the years for cleaning and safekeeping in the cathedral museum, so many of the sculptures you see here are copies.

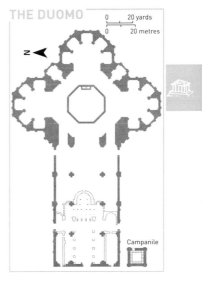

THE DUOMO

Campanile

The first tier of reliefs around the base of the tower depicts the creation of man and the arts and industries. Most were carved by **Andrea Pisano**, some supposedly after a design by Giotto; the exceptions are those of the north side (facing the cathedral), executed by **Luca della Robbia**. The reliefs of the second tier, by followers of Andrea Pisano, depict the planets, cardinal virtues, liberal arts and the seven sacraments. Above runs a band with sculptures of prophets and sybils in niches, by **Donatello** and others. At the very top are fine two- and three-light cusped windows. The bell-tower is 85 metres high and you can climb its stairs.

INTERIOR At the time it was completed the cathedral interior was a showcase of experimental ideas, designs and techniques. The new design elaborated by Francesco Talenti after 1360 radically altered the plan devised by Arnolfo di Cambio, changing the Gothic nave into a sort of luminous Imperial Roman hall whose cross vaults are borne by monumental piers with Corinthian capitals - a clear reference to the formal vocabulary of Classical antiquity. Above all in the reinvention of a 'colossal' architectural scale, the new duomo changed Italian and European sensibilities, shifting them towards the 'lost' beauty of the ancient world. The definition of the nave of Santa Maria del Fiore in just four 18-metre-wide bays (the widest of any building until that time), in place of the more minute internal division of the spaces in other great churches, underscored this new monumental approach to collective experience. The cathedral of Florence thus became the first statement since antiquity of a heroic vision of the consolidated aesthetic of a people. Such a vision could only result in a new formal language: the old altarpieces and furnishings were sold at auction, and the church was equipped with fewer but more imposing rectangular, square and circular artworks whose geometry would echo that of Classical antiquity.

THE DECORATIVE PROGRAMME The nave is lit by stained glass windows with *Saints* designed by **Agnolo Gaddi**. In the chapels of the apse and transepts are more stained glass windows, by **Ghiberti**, representing *Saints and Apostles* on the lower level and *Ancestors of Christ* above. Glazed terracottas by **Luca della Robbia** are set in the wall of the south transept and above the sacristy doors (the *Resurrection* over the door of the north sacristy, dated 1442, is his earliest major commission). The *Sacristy Door*, Luca della Robbia's only work in bronze, was a joint project with **Michelozzo** and **Maso di Bartolomeo**. Behind it lies the *Sacrestia delle Messe*, the only early-Renaissance environment in the Duomo to have survived intact, with intarsiated wood cabinets commissioned from Brunelleschi but possibly designed by Leon Battista Alberti or Paolo Uccello. A wooden *Crucifix* by Benedetto da Maiano hangs over the high altar.

The drum of the cupola has stained-glass windows representing the *Life of Christ* and the *Coronation of the Virgin*, based on designs by **Andrea del Castagno**, **Ghiberti**, **Paolo Uccello** and **Donatello**. In the dome, colourful frescoes of the *Last Judgement* by Giorgio Vasari and Federico Zuccari contrast oddly with the spareness of the buff plaster walls and grey stone trim which set the tone of the space.

In the north aisle you can see a painting by Domenico di Michelino showing *Dante Holding the Divine Comedy* which casts light on Florence, and two stunningly beautiful equestrian memorials to mercenary commanders of the Florentine army - the Englishman *Sir John Hawkwood* (left; 1436) by **Paolo Uccello**, and *Niccolò da Tolentino* (right; 1456) by **Andrea del Castagno**. Both are painted to look like sculpture, Uccello using the green *terra verde* pigment in imitation of bronze. At the west end are a mosaic of the *Coronation of the Virgin* attributed to Gaddo Gaddi, stained glass by Lorenzo Ghiberti and a *Clock Face with Four Heads of Prophets* by Paolo Uccello. The clock uses the *hora italica* method of counting the hours: the last hour of the day ends at sunset or Ave Maria.

The beautiful marble *pavement* was created in the 16c to designs by **Bacco d'Agnolo** (nave and aisles), **Cronaca** (east end) and, possibly, **Michelangelo** (crossing). Steps between the first and second south piers lead down to the excavations of the ancient cathedral of Santa Reparata.

The Museo dell' Opera

OPEN	Mon-Sat 9.00-19.30; Sun 9.00-13.40; also, 6/1, 1/11, 8/12, 26/12, 9.00-13.40
CLOSED	1/1, Easter, 25/12
CHARGES	06; ticket sales end 40 minutes before closing
TELEPHONE	**055 230 2885**
WWW.	operaduomo.firenze.it
MAIN ENTRANCE	Piazza del Duomo 9
DISABLED ACCESS	Ask at reception
GUIDED VISITS	Audio tours available
SERVICES	Bookshop

HIGHLIGHTS
Sculpture by Luca della Robbia, Donatello, Michelangelo

The Opera di Santa Maria del Fiore is a secular organization: literally, the 'Board of Works'. It was established by the Florentine Republic to oversee the construction of the new cathedral of Santa Maria del Fiore and, once its building was complete, to assure the conservation and restoration of the cathedral, campanile and baptistery. From the laying of the first stone (8 September 1296), the Opera's principal goal has been to preserve and protect the cathedral as the common heritage of all Florentines.

Among the artists represented today in the Museo dell'Opera are Andrea Pisano, Luca and Andrea della Robbia, Brunelleschi, Donatello and Michelangelo. Their masterpieces include the four seated *Evangelists* made for the old façade of the duomo by **Donatello**, his beautiful wood statue of *St Mary Magdalene*, and his fine statues from the niches of the campanile. His marble *Pulpit* (commonly called a *cantoria*, or choir loft), is displayed opposite the charming one made by **Luca della Robbia**. These exquisite works of Florentine Renaissance sculpture (both of the 1430s) were among the first furnishings executed for the cathedral after the completion of Brunelleschi's dome; they were originally located above the doors of the sacristies.

Michelangelo's *Pietà* is a late work (1547-55) intended for his own tomb. It was finished by a pupil. Michelangelo includes his own self-portrait in the figure who holds Christ - identified by the sources as Nicodemus, the old man who (according to the Gospel of St John) went by night to ask Christ how a man might be reborn. Tradition says Nicodemus was a sculptor, and this contributed to the elderly Michelangelo's deep identification with the event shown. The visual and emotional centre of this Pietà is no longer Mary (as it is in the earlier *Pietà* in St Peter's in Rome), but Jesus in the arms of Nicodemus-Michelangelo. In the pyramidal composition, the hooded Nicodemus is in the vertex.

A room contains original low reliefs from the campanile by **Andrea Pisano**. The exquisite silver-gilt *Altar* from the baptistery is a remarkable work by Florentine goldsmiths; it was finished in the 15c.

THE CIVIC CENTRE

Palazzo Vecchio

OPEN	Mon-Wed & Fri-Sun 9.00-19.00; Thurs 9.00-14.00
CLOSED	1/1, 1/5, 25/12
CHARGES	€5.70
TELEPHONE	055 276 8465
WWW.	comune.firenze.it/servizi pubblici/arte/musei/a.htm Museo dei Ragazzi: **museoragazzi.it**
MAIN ENTRANCE	Piazza della Signoria, north side; Via della Ninna
DISABLED ACCESS	Yes (ask at Reception)
GUIDED VISITS	Audio tours available
SERVICES	Bookshop, café/restaurant

Piazza della Signoria has been the centre of Florentine political life since the Middle Ages. Its history parallels that of Palazzo Vecchio, which rises austerely on the square's east side. More than any other single building, this immense stone fortress represents the essence of Florentine history. Built by Arnolfo di Cambio between 1298 and 1314, it is the traditional seat of Florentine government. Originally the residence of the *priore*, an executive nominated by the rich and powerful city guilds, it became the meeting-place of the *signoria*, Florence's first parliament, then the residence of the Medici, the family of bankers who eventually became the city's absolute rulers. The name Palazzo Vecchio ('Old Palace') was coined in the mid-16c when Duke Cosimo I de' Medici moved the family home to the more sumptuous Pitti Palace.

EXTERIOR

The **façade** has remained intact through the centuries. Made of a rusticated sandstone known as *pietra forte*, it is divided by narrow string-courses into three orders and crowned by a crenellated walkway beneath which the arms of the Commune of Florence are frescoed. Near the top of the 94m-high tower, tall arched corbels support a covered gallery and battlement with the dove-tail crenellations that denote allegiance to the Holy Roman Emperor. Above, the bell that called parliament to session in past centuries hangs between four stout columns. These carry a second crenellated battlement and the bronze spire, surmounted by a gilt lily and lion symbolic of Florence. Inside the tower is a small room, known as the *Alberghettino*, where Cosimo de' Medici the Elder, Girolamo Savonarola, and other prominent Florentines who fell from favour were imprisoned.

The main entrance is asymmetrically placed near the southwest corner of the palace. At the sides of the doorway stand statues of *Hercules and Cacus* (carved in 1534 by Bacio Bandinelli) and *David* (a modern copy of Michelangelo's famous work of 1504; the original has been removed to the Accademia); and two anthropomorphic posts that originally held a chain. On the steps are copies of Donatello's *Judith and Holofernes* and the *Marzocco* lion (originals inside, and in the Museo Nazionale del Bargello, respectively). The great *Neptune Fountain* was created between 1562 and 1575 by **Bartolomeo Ammannati** and assistants, among them the young Giambologna, who worked on the elegant bronze groups of the basin. A porphyry disk in the pavement just in front of the fountain marks the spot where Savonarola was hanged and burned at the stake in 1498, and an equestrian statue of *Cosimo de' Medici* (1595) by Giambologna stands off to one side.

Ammannati's *Neptune Fountain* (1562-75)

On the other side rises the beautiful, arched **Loggia della Signoria**, also called *Loggia dell'Orcagna* and *Loggia dei Lanzi* (from the *Lanzichenecchi*, the guards of Cosimo I who were stationed here). It was built in the 14c by Benci di Cione and Simone di Francesco Talenti after a design probably by **Andrea Orcagna**. Originally intended for public ceremonies, it has been used since the 18c as a showcase for sculptures.

To the left of the steps is Benvenuto Cellini's magnificent bronze statue of *Perseus Holding the Head of Medusa* (1584). To the right is Giambologna's *Rape of the Sabine Women* (1582), his final work and a famous Mannerist sculpture. The other sculptures are Giambologna's *Hercules and the Centaur*; a Roman copy of a Greek statue of *Ajax with the Body of Patroclos*; Pio Fede's late-19c *Rape of Polissena* and, against the rear wall, Roman statues of women. An ancient Greek lion and its Renaissance cousin flank the steps; the antique piece is on the right.

INTERIOR

The interior was entirely rebuilt in the 16c by **Giorgio Vasari** and his assistants for Cosimo I de' Medici. Most of what you see today is an overblown celebration of Florence's ruling dynasty. An example of this is the first-floor **Salone dei Cinquecento**, built in 1495 for the meetings of the Consiglio Maggiore of the Republic. The statues here memorialize the Medici family (with the exception of Michelangelo's *Victory*); the paintings, military victories and the life of Cosimo. The most charming of the 16c additions is the little **Studiolo** (1570-5), built to hold the fruits of Francesco de' Medici's scientific experiments and other rare or precious objects from the prince's collection. It is considered one of the highest expressions of Florentine Mannerism.

Two or three of the rooms built before the advent of the Medici have survived on the second floor, beyond the apartments occupied by Cosimo's consort, Eleonora di Toledo, and her children.

The **Cappella della Signoria** was originally the Cappella dei Priori. It was painted by Ridolfo del Ghirlandaio with passages drawn from the Old and New Testaments intended to serve as admonition for Florence's governors.

The **Sala dell'Udienza** was originally the courtroom of the Florentine Republic. Built between 1472 and 1481 after a design by Benedetto da Maiano, it has a superb wooden ceiling carved and gilded by Giuliano da Maiano and his assistants. A statue of *Justice* by Benedetto sits in the lunette above the doorway. The fresco decoration of the walls, painted by Franceso Salviati between 1550 and 1560, revolves around a complicated *Allegory of Justice*. Donatello's bronze statue of *Judith and Holofernes* (c 1455), formerly located on the palace steps, now stands before the central window of the left wall.

The **Sala dei Gigli**, also designed by Benedetto da Maiano, is named after the heraldic lilies of Florence that adorn its walls and ceiling, the latter beautifully carved and gilded by Giuliano da Maiano and his assistants. Over the marble doorway is a statue of *St John the Baptist* by Benedetto, while Giuliano, with Francione (Francesco di Giovanni), made the inlaid doors. The pictorial decoration is the work of Domenico Ghirlandaio and his assistants.

The **Cancelleria**, built in 1511, was Niccolò Machiavelli's office during his term as Secretary of the Republic. **Verrocchio**'s *Winged Putto*, the original removed from the fountain in the courtyard, stands in the centre of the room.

The **Sala delle Carte Geografiche** has a wooden ceiling and cabinets bearing maps begun in 1563 by Fra Ignazio Danti for Cosimo I and completed in 1581 by Stefano Buonsignori for Francesco I. They illustrate the world as it was then known and are of great historical and scientific interest. Danti also designed the globe at the centre of the room, the largest of its time.

Palazzo Vecchio is also home to a new children's museum, the **Museo dei Ragazzi** with hands-on activities.

The Uffizi

OPEN	Tues-Sun 8.15-18.50
	(**Vasari Corridor**: groups by appointment only)
CLOSED	Mon, 1/1, 1/5, 25/12
CHARGES	Full price €6.50, booking (optional) €1.55.
	Ticket sales end 45 minutes before closing
	50% reduction for 18-25-year-olds from the EU and for accredited teachers. Admission is free for young people under 18, school groups (participants must be listed on school letterhead), accredited journalists, those accompanying the disabled and EU citizens over 60
TELEPHONE	055 238 8651/652; booking and information, 055 294 883
WWW.	uffizi.firenze.it; firenzemusei.it
MAIN ENTRANCE	Piazzale degli Uffizi 6: Door 4 (reserved visitors), Door 5 (unreserved visitors)
DISABLED ACCESS	Yes (ask at Reception)
GUIDED VISITS	Guided visits can be organized by contacting the Education Department of the Curator's Office (**T** 055 238 8658) or the booking service (**T** 055 294 883)
SERVICES	Cloakroom, information desk, café, two museum shops (with outside access), multimedia room

The Uffizi

The Galleria degli Uffizi was one of the first museums in Europe to assert the modern idea of a museum as a systematically organized exhibition space designed for public viewing. The building was commissioned from Vasari in 1560 by Cosimo I de' Medici to house his duchy's administrative and judicial offices - *uffizi* in old Italian. Five years later Vasari was engaged again, to build an overhead corridor connecting the Uffizi to the new Medici residence at Palazzo Pitti. But it is to Cosimo's son, Francesco I (1541-87), that the first real nucleus of the Uffizi Gallery owes its origin. This introverted Medici scion had already established a Studiolo filled with paintings and precious objects in his residence in the Palazzo Vecchio. Around 1581 he hired the eclectic Bernardo Buontalenti to turn the top floor of the Uffizi into a gallery where he could 'stroll amidst paintings, statues and other precious things'.

   Nowadays the Uffizi Gallery displays nearly 2000 paintings from the medieval to the modern age, together with ancient sculptures, miniatures, and tapestries. So many masterpieces are collected here that it's barely possible to skate over the surface in a single visit; it makes sense to limit your initial tour to a few outstanding works. The collections are reached by the monumental Grand Staircase.

HIGHLIGHTS

Giotto, *Maestà*   Room 2

Paolo Uccello, *Battle of San Romano*   Room 7
Piero della Francesca, *Diptych of the Duke
and Duchess of Urbino*

Fra' Filippo Lippi, *Madonna with Child and Two Angels*	Room 8
Botticelli, including the *Primavera*	Rooms 10-14
Leonardo da Vinci, *Annunciation*	Room 15
Michelangelo, *Holy Family* (*Doni Tondo*)	Room 25
Raphael, *Madonna of the Goldfinch* and *Pope Leo X with Cardinals Giulio de' Medici and Luigi de' Rossi*	Room 26
Titian, *Venus of Urbino*	Room 28
Caravaggio, *Sacrifice of Isaac*	Room 43

EAST CORRIDOR

The corridors faithfully reflect Francesco I's original designs. Portraits of historical figures have been placed at the top of the walls, by the ceiling; the series was begun for Cosimo I by Cristofano dell'Altissimo, who between 1552 and 1509 copied a renowned collection by Paolo Giovio in Como. Below are large three-quarter-length portraits commissioned by Francesco I and his successors to extol their family, beginning with the founder, Giovanni di Bicci de' Medici. Ancient busts and sculptures from the Medici collection alternate along the walls. The *grotteschi* decorations were executed in fresco with tempera retouches in 1581 by a group of painters led by Alessandro Allori.

GIOTTO AND THE 13C *Room 2* Alongside some early examples of Tuscan painting, this room houses three imposing *Maestàs* - paintings of the Virgin Mary in her role as Queen of Heaven, presenting the Christ Child to the faithful. Intended as altarpieces, these large devotional images show the roots of Florentine and Sienese painting as they were to flower over the next 200 years.

Cimabue's *Maestà*, on the right wall, was painted between 1280 and 1290 for the church of Santa Trìnita. Eight foreshortened angels flank the Mother and Child; below, at the corners of the

UFFIZI GALLERY

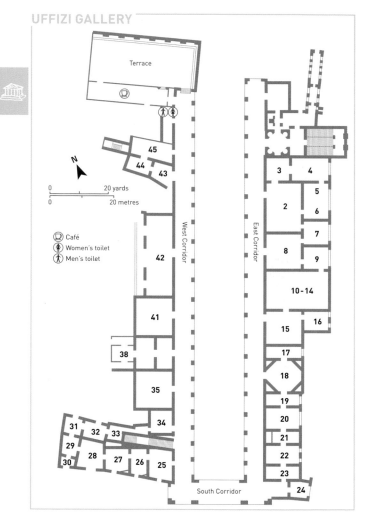

Terrace

45

44 43

N

0 — 20 yards
0 — 20 metres

Café
Women's toilet
Men's toilet

West Corridor

East Corridor

42

41

38

35

34

31

32 33

29

30 28   27 26 25

3   4

5

2   6

7

8   9

10–14

15 16

17

18

19

20

21

22

23

24

South Corridor

throne, Jeremiah and Isaiah look up at the living confirmation of their prophecies foretelling the virgin birth of Jesus, while Abraham and David, from whose lineage the Saviour comes, stand pensively beneath the central arch.

Duccio di Boninsegna's *Maestà* from Santa Maria Novella, on the left wall, dates from around 1285 and is the Sienese painter's first known large work. Like Cimabue's altarpiece, it shows the static quality typical of the Byzantine tradition - a tradition that could claim direct descendancy from Imperial Roman art. A curious detail is the way the painting continues on the frame: the six kneeling angels that surround the Virgin and Child provide a transition between the One (God) and the many (us), represented by the thirty saints and half-length biblical figures portrayed in medallions around the image.

At the centre of the room rises **Giotto**'s extraordinary *Maestà* (c 1310), painted for the church of Ognissanti. Nowhere are the virginity, maternity, and royalty of Mary more clearly expressed than in this image, which was to leave a lasting mark on art in Florence and throughout Europe. The Virgin smiles ever so slightly, the folds of her garments fall naturally over her body. At the sides of the meticulously constructed throne an angel offers Mary the crown of heaven; another gives Jesus the eucharistic pyx, a symbol of the Passion. Angels kneeling at the foot of the throne offer vases with roses and lilies, both Marian symbols. Everywhere the figures are solidly arranged and the space clearly defined, giving rise to a sense of reality of life that is echoed in the naturalism of the faces, of the variegated marble, of the flowers painted from nature and even of the wood of the platform beneath the Virgin's feet.

SIENESE PAINTING OF THE 14C *Room 3.* Here is a lovely *Annunciation* by Simone Martini and Lippo Memmi, signed and dated 1333. It is typical of Sienese sensibility in its fine use of gold and its linearity. Gabriel's greeting is written into the gold ground behind the carefully rendered lily.

EARLY FLORENTINE RENAISSANCE PAINTING *Room 7* One of
the more fascinating paintings of the early Renaissance is
Masaccio and **Masolino**'s 1424 collaboration, *St Anne Metterza* from
the church of Sant'Ambrogio. The Virgin, her mother and her Child
are placed along a central, vertical axis, giving the composition
the static quality of Byzantine altarpieces but with a sense of
natural, three-dimensional volume. The term *metterza* ('third in a
series', roughly translated from ecclesiastical Latin) is often used
in reference to representations showing the mother of the Virgin
with her daughter and the Child. In this painting St Anne acquires
a key symbolic value: to the faithful she represents a mother who
protects a daughter who is without sin and who is the progenitress
of the body of Christ.

The most impressive painting in the room is certainly **Paolo
Uccello**'s *Battle of San Romano*, which came to the Uffizi from
Lorenzo il Magnifico's chambers in the Medici Palace on Via
Larga, now Via Cavour. It is known to be one of several panels
showing phases of the battle - two others are in the Louvre in
Paris and the National Gallery in London. The victory owed much
to Lorenzo's father, Cosimo il Vecchio, and to his cousin Averado,
who were both financial backers of the Florentine expedition;
contemporaries would surely have recognized the message it bore
regarding the Medici's place in public life. The spectacular clash
of horsemen focuses on the unsaddling of Bernardino della
Ciarda, leader of the enemy army. In what may be the most
provocative image of warfare of all time, Paolo Uccello reveals his
almost fanatic love for the study of perspective and geometric
forms, creating a metaphysical abstraction whose sense of
unreality is heightened by the livid lighting of the figures, horses
and objects against the dark landscape background.

Domenico Veneziano's *Santa Lucia dei Magnoli Altarpiece*, dated
1445, is another masterpiece of its time and one of the few extant
works by this Venetian painter who died a pauper in Florence.
Painted in pale pastel colours bathed in unusually soft, early-
morning light, it abandons the traditional medieval triptych form
for a harmonious architectural structure of three arches made
ever the more precious by receding squares of polychrome marble

in the floor and delicate citrus trees in the background. St Francis, St John the Baptist, St Zanobius and St Lucy mediate the viewer's approach to the Mother in Child in a compositional type that would come to be known as a Sacred Conversation.

Among the smaller works in this room is **Piero della Francesca**'s famous *Diptych of the Duke and Duchess of Urbino*, painted in 1467-70. Originally joined by a hinge, double portraits of this sort were often given as gifts in the 15c. It shows here forebears, Duke Federigo II da Montefeltro and his wife Battista Sforza facing one another in solemn profile, in the Classical medallion style popular during the Humanist period. The figures are immersed in an atmosphere of crystalline purity and bathed in a diffuse morning light. The precision of the features, focusing even on the less attractive details (Federigo's nose was chipped in a tournament), and of the meticulously rendered landscape background establishes the painter as one of the more sensitive interpreters of Northern European art, which was just coming into vogue at this time. The rear panels, with the *Allegorical Triumphs of Battista Sforza and Federigo da Montefeltro*, are inspired by Petrarch's 14c poetical *Triumphs*. They indicate the subjects' moral integrity. Each spouse is solemnly accompanied on a triumphal carriage by four virtues: the theological virtues (Faith, Charity, Hope and Modesty) for Battista and the cardinal virtues (Prudence, Temperance, Fortitude and Justice) for Federigo. Battista's carriage is drawn by unicorns, symbols of purity and chastity; and Federigo is crowned by Victory.

FILIPPO AND FILIPPINO LIPPI *Room 8* Filippo Lippi is an interesting person. He was a Carmelite monk, and he modelled his enchanting Madonnas after Lucrezia Buti, the beautiful blonde nun with whom he was madly - and scandalously - in love. His chief patron and protector, Cosimo il Vecchio, in defence of his transgressive protégé, once wrote that 'great minds are heavenly forms and not dray horses for hire'; and Filippo's *Madonna with Child and Two Angels* (c 1465), the outstanding masterpiece in this room, certainly bears him out. Mary, her hair entwined with precious pearls and covered by the most ethereal of veils, her hands folded and her gaze abstracted in meditative prayer, embodies a beauty that is as much a moral as it is a physical trait. The lively, restless Infant seeks his mother's gaze and embrace with remarkable naturalism. Mother and Child are seated before a window affording a view over a landscape comprising plains, distant mountains, a city and a bay - Marian symbols that appear again and again in Renaissance Madonnas. The elegance of Filippo's vision is evident not only in the delicacy of his physical ideal but in the refinement of the costume, rendered with painstaking detail; it reflects the new Quattrocento taste, as far from Masaccio's harsh effects of light and shadow as it is from the solemnity of a bygone way of life. The artist's contemporaries were well aware of the revolutionary nature of his vision: his command of light, colour and line may have inspired Botticelli, who worked for a while as Filippo's assistant; and the background, a magnificent painting-within-a-painting, seems to lay the foundations for the landscapes of Leonardo.

Lucrezia presented Filippo with a son, later to become the gifted painter **Filippino Lippi**. He is represented here by a *Madonna with Child and Saints* (1486) and *Adoration of the Magi* (1496).

ANDREA AND PIERO DEL POLLAIOLO *Room 9* Antonio and Piero del Polliaolo ran a prolific Florentine workshop that specialized in painting, sculpture and goldsmithery. Their stunning altarpiece of 1466-8, depicting *St Jacob, St Vincent and St Eustace*, was made for the chapel of the Cardinal of Portugal in the church of San Miniato al Monte. It epitomizes the three arts for which they were famous - not only by its own physical presence, but in the richness of the saints' garments, the refinement of their architectural setting, and the astonishing atmospheric perspective of the landscape that stretches away into the distance. It is one of the first Florentine paintings to use pigments dissolved in oil - a technique pioneered by Flemish artists.

The same sense of refinement is evident in Antonio's *Portrait of a Lady*, painted (in traditional tempera technique) around 1475. The subject is shown in half-bust profile against a rich background of blue lapis lazuli. Around her neck is a pearl necklace with a particularly beautiful pendant, which shows an angel in relief overlying a large ruby. Her dress is richly brocaded and she is wearing the same Quattrocento headdress worn by Fra' Filippo Lippi's Madonna: a wondrously delicate veil held in place over her tightly plaited golden hair by a string of pearls.

BOTTICELLI *Rooms 10-14* Botticell is best known for his *Primavera* and its companion piece, the *Birth of Venus* - sublime mythological allegories painted for the Medici and inspired by the Neoplatonic currents that pervaded their intellectual circle.

The Primavera

A fascinating and enigmatic work, the *Primavera* was probably painted for Lorenzo di Pierfrancesco de' Medici, a second cousin of Lorenzo il Magnifico. No one knows exactly when it was done; scholars have dated it roughly to the late 1470s or early 1480s.

The scene is set in a luxuriant garden, strewn with minutely rendered flowers and plants. Beneath the closely planted trees grow sprigs of myrtle, which form a natural halo behind the central figure. This white-robed woman is the obvious protagonist of the image. She is shown to be Aphrodite by the myrtle, which ancient mythographers associated with the goddess. Consequently the grove in which the action takes place can be identified as Aphrodite's sacred garden, which Greek myth placed on the isle of Cyprus.

Hovering over Aphrodite's head, blind Love prepares to shoot a flaming arrow at the outermost of the three young women who join hands in the circular dance of the Graces. Their rhythmic movements, frozen in the painterly representation, convey a fair-haired, slender-bodied beauty that was canonic in the 15c. Their sheer garments, which break with the Greco-Roman tradition of showing the Graces nude, signify the sincerity, honesty and tangibility of those moral values which the young women represent and the circulation of which is perpetuated by their embrace.

At the extreme left of the painting, clothed only in a red mantle, is Hermes, messenger of the gods and guardian of the sacred grove. With his raised caduceus he disperses a bank of intrusive clouds, which threaten to disturb the eternal spring of the garden.

On the right of the painting a young woman draped with garlands of roses and myrtle strews rosebuds over the ground in front of her as she walks. They blossom here and there around her, establishing that it is she who brings to the garden the scents and colours of spring. Her position in the narrative associates her with the sexual union that is consummated at the extreme right of the garden. Here Zephyr, the west wind that announces the coming of spring, bursts from the dark wood to seize the nymph Chloris, who flees him in terror.

The story is told in Ovid's *Fasti* (V, 193-212), a transposition in rhyme of the Roman calendar. The fertile, if forced, encounter of Zephyr and the nymph generates the first fruits of spring, which Ovid says flow miraculously from her mouth. Zephyr, to make ammends for his empassioned assault, takes Chloris as his bride, presenting her as a wedding gift with the eternal youth of spring and giving her absolute power over flowers. Chloris, elevated by her marriage to the rank of goddess, takes charge of the germinal processes of all floral species; in her new role she is Flora, the Roman goddess of youth and plant life, the deity of sowing time and protectress of female fertility.

Botticelli has translated Ovid's tale into a painterly allegory of the beneficial action of the wind which brings the first warmth of spring and urges the seed to sprout and grow, reconciling Christianity and natural philosophies. The *Primavera* in this light would appear as a cosmological-spiritual representation of universal cyclicity, where fecundating Zephyr joins with Flora to 'denote' Spring, symbol of the generative powers of Nature. At the centre Aphrodite/Venus, identified with *Humanitas* - the complex of man's spiritual activities - directs the concordant action of the Graces, which represent the operative moment of this activity. On the left Hermes/Mercury, symbol of reason and good council, watches over the harmonious fulfilment of the cycle, carefully dissipating the clouds of passion and intemperance.

This large room also contains works by Botticelli's contemporaries. In **Domenico Ghirlandaio**'s *Madonna Enthroned with Angels and Saints* of c 1480, against the background of a crystal clear sky, a balustrade covered in jewels supports the enthroned Virgin, surrounded by four garlanded angels. The other figures are archangels Michael and Raphael, standing, St Giusto (patron saint of the church for which the painting was made) and St Zanobius. Vasari praised the metallic brilliance of the Archangel Michael's armour, obtained not through the application of gold but with pure colour, an innovation first attributable to this artist. Ghirlandaio was one of the main artists to take an interest in the novelties of Flemish art, the influences of which can be seen in his landscapes and his special attention to decorative detail.

Hugo van der Goes' large *Portinari Triptych* (c 1477-8) was painted in Bruges for Tommaso Portinari, an agent of the Medici and councillor of the Duchy of Burgundy. In this great triptych the patron and his spouse, Maria Maddalena Baroncelli, are portrayed on the side panels, absorbed in prayer before the Adoration of the Shepherds, with patron saints and the eldest of their ten children, Maria, Antonio and Pigello. The extreme naturalism of the altarpiece, facilitated by the transparency and brilliance of oil paint, left an indelible mark on Italian Renaissance painting.

LEONARDO DA VINCI *Room 15* This room documents the early years of **Leonardo**'s activity in Florence, from his beginnings in Verrocchio's studio to his departure for Milan in 1482. Also exhibited here are paintings by Leonardo's master, Andrea del Verrocchio, and his contemporaries Perugino and Piero di Cosimo.

Verrocchio's *Baptism of Christ* was painted around 1475-8 for the church of San Michele in San Salvi. Contemporary sources suggest the adolescent Leonardo made the angel in profile and the landscape background that gently fades into the distance; that the painting shows several different styles suggests that other pupils had a hand in its making, too.

Leonardo's *Annunciation* was painted for the church of San Bartolomeo a Oliveto between 1475 and 1480, when the artist was still a youth. With its restoration in 2000, its luminosity and clarity of detail has been fully revealed and its sense of perspective heightened by the view now offered by the interior of the room on the right. The composition is quite erudite: the Virgin is shown not in her room, where she is described in scripture, but in a walled garden symbolic both of paradise (the word derives from the ancient Persian for 'enclosed garden') and of her Virgin womb and its 'fruit', Jesus. The flowers in the foreground, studied from nature, form an authentic botanic garden, and the magnificent landscape background contains all the Marian elements of sea, city and mountain. The early morning light in which the artist has chosen to describe the event reveals a clear symbolic intent.

TRIBUNE *Room 18* This wonderful example of late Mannerist interior design was created by **Bernardo Buontalenti** between 1584 and 1601 for Francesco I, and like the Studiolo in the Palazzo Vecchio it was intended to hold special treasures. The octagonal room symbolizes the cosmos and its elements, the lantern with its wind rose represents air; the ceiling, made of mother-of-pearl shells set into a ground of lapis lazuli, water; the red velvet walls, fire; the marble and the semi-precious stones of the floor, earth.

The most famous is the *Medici Venus*, a Roman copy after a Greek original of the 2c BC, discovered at Hadrian's Villa in Tivoli. Other antique works include the *Young Apollo*, derived from a 4c BC Apollo by Praxiteles, described by Lucian; the *Knife Grinder* (now believed to be a Scythian awaiting Apollo's order to flay Marsyas) and the *Wrestlers*, both copies of originals by the school of Pergamum; and the *Dancing Faun*, a 3c Greek copy of an original by Praxiteles (and actually a satyr, not a faun).

The walls are hung with a spectacular series of court portraits. Among the more outstanding are **Pontormo**'s *Portrait of Cosimo il Vecchio* (c 1519-20), painted posthumously and portraying the subject in profile; **Andrea del Sarto**'s *Young Woman with a Book of Petrarch* (c 1528), where the sitter smiles mysteriously as she points to the verses of two love poems by Petrarch; **Bronzino**'s stunning portrait in red and gold of *Lucrezia Panciatichi* (c 1541) and his rather more staid *Eleonora di Toledo with Her Son Giovanni* (c 1545).

Tucked away somewhat incongruously among all these figures of power and wealth is one of the best-loved images in Western art, **Rosso Fiorentino**'s *Angel Musician* of 1521, probably part of an altarpiece with the Virgin and Saints of which all trace has been lost.

PERUGINO AND SIGNORELLI *Room 19* The *Portrait of a Young Man* painted by Pietro Peugino after 1494 is believed to be modelled on his pupil Raphael. **Luca Signorelli**'s *Madonna and Child* (1484–90), with its nudes in the background, was to become the inspiration for **Michelangelo**'s famous '*Doni Tondo*' (Room 25). Not to be missed in this room is **Lorenzo di Credi**'s little *Annunciation* of 1480–5, a remarkably delicate oil painting with a fine landscape background and a faux frieze of reliefs telling the story of Adam and Eve.

GERMAN PAINTING *Room 20* This and the next four rooms have ceilings frescoed in 1588 by Ludovico Buti; Room 20 is decorated with views of Florentine spectacles (heavily repainted in the 19c). The room is hung with masterpieces by the great German painters Albrecht Dürer and Lukas Cranach the Elder, and by the Flemish painter Pieter Bruegel the Elder. **Dürer**'s *Adoration of the Magi* (1504), painted after the artist's first trip to Italy (1494) and before his second (1505), shows a sense of colour and composition reminiscent of Venetian painting. **Cranach**'s two-panel depiction of *Adam and Eve* before their sin, signed and dated 1528, shows the parents of humankind as beautiful Classical nudes. Based on a famous etching made by Dürer in 1504, it is one of several representations the artist made of this subject.

GIOVANNI BELLINI AND GIORGIONE *Room 21* **Giovanni Bellini** produced this *Sacred Allegory* some time between 1487 and 1501. Never satisfactorily explained, it remains one of the more enigmatic works of Western painting. A curious assembly of figures and animals (including a centaur) inhabit a peaceful aquatic landscape. In the foreground is a kind of enclosed terrace on which the seated Virgin is flanked by two women while a child (possibly St John) offers the Infant Jesus (the only other figure who is seated) an apple from a tree (the Tree of Life?) being shaken by a playmate at the centre of the composition, where the inlaid stones of the pavement form a cross. St Jerome (or Job) and St Sebastian stand off to the right; at the balustrade St Paul drives away a stranger while St Peter (or St Joseph) watches over the children. On the opposite shore is St Anthony's hermitage, marked by a cross. Scholars have suggested the painting represents an allegory of Redemption, or of Life.

More arcane meaning pervades the two small panels by **Giorgione** and his pupils, *Moses Undergoing Trial by Fire* (c 1502-5) and *The Judgement of Solomon* (c 1502-8). The episode of the trial by fire, narrated in medieval Jewish texts such as the *Shermot Rabbà*, shows Pharoah testing the infant Moses by exposing him to burning coals; in the companion piece, drawn from the Bible (I *Kings*), Pharoah's place is taken by Solomon, who arbitrates between two women who contest a living child while disowning another child, dead on the ground. Both scenes are set against the mysterious idyllic landscapes typical of Giorgione's art.

THE FLEMISH AND GERMAN RENAISSANCE *Room 22* Flemish painting returns in Room 22 with two fine *Portraits* by **Hans Memling**, painted roughly 20 years apart (c 1470 and 1490) and probably depicting members of the Portinari family. Memling, one of the more accomplished portraitists of his time, left a profound mark on Italian artists, particularly Perugino. The room's other great portrait, **Hans Holbein the Younger**'s *Portrait of Sir Richard Southwell*, was presented as a gift in 1620 to Cosimo II de' Medici by Thomas Howard, Duke of Arundel. Dated 1536, it belongs to the mature phase of the English court portraitist's career and demonstrates his reputation for scrupulous accuracy.

MANTEGNA AND CORREGGIO *Room 23* The last of the rooms off the East Corridor, the former Armoury, today is dedicated to two non-Tuscan masters - Correggio of Parma and Mantegna of Padua - and painters of their circles. Three paintings by **Andrea Mantegna** - the *Adoration of the Magi*, *Ascension* and *Circumcision* - all painted after 1462 and in the Medici collections since 1587, were arbitrarily assembled in the 19c to form a triptych. They were probably part of the decoration of the chapel of San Giorgio in the Ducal Palace in Mantua. They show Mantegna's famous command of colour and composition, as well as his interest in the Classical revival brought to Northern Italy from Florence by Donatello, who worked in Padua, and Alberti, active in Mantua.

Correggio's *Virgin Adoring the Christ Child* of 1524-6 was a gift from the Duke of Mantua to Cosimo II de' Medici (1617). Painted before Correggio's famous frescoes in the cathedral of Parma, it shows a remarkable sense of light and shadow and a masterful command of atmospheric perspective.

SOUTH AND WEST CORRIDORS

With its large glass windows overlooking the Piazza degli Uffizi and the Arno River, the South Corridor is famous for its views. Some of the best pieces of sculpture are displayed here: the Hellenistic head of the *Dying Alexander* and the Roman copy of *Cupid and Psyche*, the *Boy with a Thorn in His Foot*, a replica of the 'Spinario' in the Capitoline Museum in Rome; the *Crouching Venus* and *Seated Girl Preparing to Dance*, both from Hellenistic originals of the 3c BC and, at the beginning of the West Corridor, two statues of *Marsyas*, from Hellenistic originals of the 3c BC. Above the windows facing the river are more portraits of the Giovio Series, which continue into the West Corridor together with larger paintings, including 50 portraits of the Lorraine dynasty. The famous *Wild Boar* has been reinstalled at the end of the corridor towards the Loggia dei Lanzi. This, along with the small replica of a Farnese *Hercules*, is placed beside the *Laocoön* by Baccio Bandinelli (1523), the first copy from the original Hellenistic group found in Rome in 1506.

MICHELANGELO AND FLORENTINE PAINTING *Room 25* The first of eleven rooms dedicated to 16c painting, Room 25 is dominated by Michelangelo's famous *Holy Family with the Infant St John the Baptist* (*Doni Tondo*) of 1506-8. Considered the most important and enigmatic painting of the 16c, the *Doni Tondo* is the only example of

Michelangelo *Doni Tondo* (1506-8)

Michelangelo's painting preserved in Florence. Executed for the Florentine merchant Agnolo Doni and his wife Maddalena Strozzi, possibly on the occasion of the birth of their daughter Maria (8 September 1507), it was certainly painted after January 1506 when the *Laocoön* was found in Rome - from that sculpture Michelangelo took the pose of the nude sitting behind St Joseph. The postures of the other nudes are likewise derived from Classical statuary, which the artist is known to have studied with great care.

As in his sculptures, Michelangelo has infused the figures of

Jesus, Mary and Joseph with a dynamic, twisting power that threatens to dissolve the bonds between the figures. The form is constrained in a complex system of lines and its sculptural quality is enhanced by a play of coloured lights and shadows that takes advantage both of direct light and of reflected light in the areas of shadow. The skin surfaces consequently appear as lucid as polished marble and the drapery acquires an almost metallic brilliance. The striking tones of the painting and its strangely serpentine composition sparked the trend that came to be known as Mannerism.

RAPHAEL AND ANDREA DEL SARTO *Room 26* Michelangelo is a tough act to follow, but **Raphael** proves equal to the task. His portrait of *Pope Leo X with Cardinals Giulio de' Medici and Luigi de' Rossi* arrived in Florence from Rome in 1518. Painted just a few months before the artist's death, it is one of his great masterpieces. Vasari praised it for the skilled rendering of the figures and fabrics, and for the ingenious effects of light (especially on the golden knob on the chair, which reflects the windows, the Pope's shoulders, and the surrounding room). But perhaps more important is the supreme harmony of the composition and the artist's magnificent ability to penetrate the psychology of his sitters. The figure of the pope, even in the calmness of the pose, is truly an image of power and sovereignty. The warm lighting and the symphony of deep reds, whites and golds it creates, would exert a profound influence on Titian.

The same room contains **Andrea del Sarto**'s most famous altarpiece, the *Madonna of the Harpies*, signed and dated 1517. The work derives its name from Vasari's misinterpretation of the low relief on the base. It now appears that the 'harpies' are locusts alluding to the ninth chapter of the Apocalypse. The saints are Francis and John the Evangelist; the latter is thought to be a self-portrait of the artist, whose delicate colours, elegant forms and perfect compositions won him the epitaph, 'painter without errors'.

TITIAN AND SEBASTIANO DEL PIOMBO *Room 28* **Titian**'s *Venus of Urbino* was brought to Florence in 1631 with the inheritance of

Victoria della Rovere, wife of Ferdinando II de' Medici. Commissioned from the Venetian master in 1538 by Guidubaldo della Rovere, Duke of Urbino, this is one of the more famous erotic images of all time. A young girl with loosely flowing blonde hair looks knowingly and allusively at the spectator. More than nude, she is naked, lying on a luxurious bed with rumpled sheets, her left hand half hiding, half caressing, her sex. Her right hand holds a small bouquet of roses, a love symbol reiterated by the myrtle (plant of Venus) on the window-sill. The little dog sleeping on the bed symbolizes fidelity, and an air of domestic tranquillity pervades the background, where two maid-servants look for clothes in a rich bridal chest while the sun sets outside. The artist's palette, restricted to the warmest of tones, and his close attention to the details of fabrics, flesh and even the pearl earring on the ear of the young model, identified as Giulia Varano, the duke's bride, are exquisite.

EMILIAN PAINTING *Rooms 29-30* The best work of the Emilian School artists displayed in these rooms is certainly **Parmigianino**'s famous *Madonna of the Long Neck*, begun between 1534 and 1539 for the Servite monks in Parma and never completed. On the foundations of Correggio's intellectualism Parmigianino builds an image of extreme refinement whose elongated, supple figures carry Mannerism to heights it would never reach again.

VENETIAN PAINTING *Rooms 31-32* Paolo Veronese's warm colours and vibrant lyricism sets the tone in these rooms; particularly striking are the *Holy Family* of 1561, dominated by the beautiful and sensuous figure of St Barbara. Veronese's contemporary Tintoretto is represented by a mysterious *Leda and the Swan* (c 1550-60), where the metamorphosed Zeus is accompanied by a number of other 'pets': a parrot in a cage, a cat staring menacingly at a duck in a crate and Leda's lap-dog, who clearly doesn't approve of the swan's intentions.

LOMBARD PAINTING *Room 34* The best-known artist of the Lombard School, **Lorenzo Lotto** was an intellectual and a loner.

His little panel representing the *Chastity of Susannah*, signed and dated 1517, transforms the biblical episode of Susannah being harassed by two old men while bathing into a strange fairy-tale. The scene is shown from above to reveal an apparently idyllic background behind Susannah's walled courtyard; but close examination reveals two voyeurs hidden in the branches of a tree, spying on Susannah as she walks to the bath. The scrolls held by the principal actors hold the texts of what would be their lines if this were theatre: Susannah says she does not want to sin; the resentful intruders accuse her of adultery with a young man.

CORRIDOIO VASARIANO

Between Rooms 25 and 34 is the stair leading to the Corridoio Vasariano, to visit which you must make an appointment. In 1565, when Francesco I married Joanna of Austria, the Medici commissioned Vasari to build the corridor to join the Uffizi to Palazzo Pitti, passing over the Ponte Vecchio and Via Guicciardini in such a manner that the archdukes could make their rounds without rubbing elbows with their subjects. The *corridoio* offers interesting views of Florence and has been hung with a celebrated collection of artists' self-portraits, beginning with Vasari himself and continuing, in chronological order, past the Gaddis and Raphael to Rembrandt, Van Dyck, Velázquez, Hogarth, Reynolds, Delacroix, Corot and others.

RUBENS *Room 41* **Pieter Paul Rubens'** touching *Portrait of Isabella Brandt* (c 1625), his first wife, is a fitting introduction to the 17c European works displayed in this room. Isabella, 'completely good, completely honest and beloved for her virtues' died in 1626; often portrayed by the artist, she is shown here half length, smiling gently, in a composition whose tone is set by warm tones of red and brown

Diego Velázquez and his workshop executed the magnificent portrait of *Philip IV of Spain on Horseback* around 1645 after a composition by Rubens (c 1628) known from a description but destroyed in Madrid in 1734. The king was 22 years old in the original, but Velázquez has here borrowed his face from a later portrait, today in the Frick Collection in New York.

COLLECTIONS OF THE 17C AND 18C *Rooms 43-44* Room 43 has three sensational paintings by **Caravaggio**: the early *Medusa* (c 1592-1600), the famous *Bacchus* (1596-1600) and the influential *Sacrifice of Isaac*, variously dated from 1592 to 1604. In this great painting Caravaggio shows the angel staying Abraham's hand as he prepares to slay his son Isaac in obedience to God. (The ram who will substitute Isaac approaches unsuspecting from the right.) As the story is told in the Book of Genesis, the angel does not intervene physically, but merely speaks to Abraham from the heavens. The painting, with its signature effects of light and shadow and its serene, Venetian-type landscape background, concords with the new spirituality of the Counter-Reformation: the sacrifice of Isaac prefigures that of Christ, and Abraham's obedience embodies the virtue of unwavering faith.

   Superb command of light and shadow also distinguish **Rembrandt**'s *Self-portrait as a Young Man*, an early painting (c 1634) already full of self-confidence and psychological insight; **Canaletto**'s *View of the Ducal Palace in Venice* (before 1755), where mathematical and atmospheric perspective combine to create a singular impression of naturalism; **Giambattista Tiepolo**'s daringly illusionistic *Erection of a Statue to an Emperor* (1735-6) from the archiepiscopal seminary of Udine; and **Goya**'s stunning *Portrait of María Teresa, Countess of Chinchón* (c 1798), one of the many paintings Goya made of the daughter of his patron, Louís de Borbón, who like the artist died in exile in France.

The exit from the gallery is between Rooms 35 and 41, but the café at the end of the West Corridor gives access to the rooftop terrace of the Loggia della Signoria, worth visiting for its spectacular views over the square.

on route

Fiorentina Antica offers a rare opportinuty to explore an early palace interior and to learn about domestic life in the 14c-16c. Closed for restoration at the time of writing. For information: Firenze Musei, *T* 055 282 828 (9.00-19.00).

Mercato Nuovo This arched loggia, designed by Giovanni Battista del Tasso for Cosimo I in 1547, was intended for the sale of gold and silk. It is now a market for straw work, leather goods, and other handicrafts.

Museo di Storia della Scienza, Piazza dei Giudici. Open daily except Tues 9.30-13.00 in winter; 9.30-17.00 and Sat 9.30-13.00 in summer. €6.50, *T* 055 239 8876. Although you won't find exciting hands-on displays and fascinating experiments demonstrating the principles of physics and chemistry, you will be treated to an intriguing array of antique scientific instruments. Here are Arabian astrolabes and Tuscan sundials, gigantic armillary spheres, two of Galileo's original telescopes and the lens with which he discovered the moons of Jupiter.

Orsanmichele, Via Calzaiuoli. Half-way between the duomo and Palazzo Vecchio stands the church of Orsanmichele. Heresay has it that Arnolfo di Cambio built a covered marketplace, much like the present strawmarket (see above), on this site in 1290, but that it was destroyed by fire in 1304. In 1337 the architects Francesco Talenti, Neri di Fioravante and Benci di Cione began the building you see today.

The main façade, on the side opposite Via Calzaiuoli, has two beautiful doors by Niccolò di Lamberti (1410). Built into the perimetral piers are tabernacles carrying statues commissioned by the guilds of Florence from prominent artists, including Donatello, Ghiberti and Verrocchio. All the statues are labelled in Italian and English; some have been removed for restoration, and others have been replaced by copies.

Palazzo dell'Arte della Lana An elevated walkway connects Orsanmichele to the Palazzo dell'Arte della Lana, built in 1308 for the Woolworkers' Guild, which in the 13c employed 30,000 of Florence's 90,000 inhabitants in roughly 300 woollen industries.

Palazzo Davanzati, Piazza Davanzati, is the best preserved 14c palace in Florence. Inside, the **Museo della Casa Fiorentina Antica** offers a rare opportinuty to explore an early palace interior and to learn about domestic life in the 14c-16c. Closed for restoration at the time of writing. For information: Firenze Musei, *T* 055 282 828 (9.00-19.00).

Palazzo Strozzi

Palazzo Strozzi, Piazza Strozzi. **Benedetto da Maiano**'s townhouse for banker Filippo Strozzi (1489-1536) differs from all examples of the Medici palace type in its use of rustication, so slightly graduated from one storey to the next as to seem uniform throughout. The oblong courtyard is the finest in Florence.

Ponte Vecchio With its quaint old houses, the Ponte Vecchio is a famous sight of Florence. It was the only bridge over the Arno until 1218, and it has been reconstructed many times. The design of the present bridge, attributed to Taddeo Gaddi or to Neri di Fioravante, dates from the 14c. An edict of 1593 established that all the existing butchers' and grocers' shops should be replaced by those of goldsmiths - an important trade in Florence. Many prominent artists - including Brunelleschi, Ghiberti and Donatello - were trained as goldsmiths; but the most distinguished of all was Benvenuto Cellini, honoured here with a modern bust.

The Ponte Vecchio

commercial galleries

Isabella Brancolini, Lungarno Acciaiuoli 4, *T* 055 281 549. In business in her own space since 2002, Isabella Brancolini has curated the exhibitions at the Gallery Hotel Art since 1998; Italian and international contemporary art, with an emphasis on photography.

eating and drinking

There is a dire lack of good restaurants in Florence's city centre, though the area is home to several good wine bars. These are places where you can enjoy a delicious light lunch, and buy wine and special foods to take home, too. Downtown Florence also abounds in good cafés.

AT THE MUSEUMS

€ **Galleria degli Uffizi**, *T* 055 238 8651/652. At the end of the west corridor, with a sunny terrace on the roof of the Loggia della Signoria, this museum café serves coffee, snacks and light lunches in the most panoramic setting in the city.

Palazzo Vecchio. The museum café is tucked away behind the ticket office in a dull, remote part of the building. You'll be better off seeking refreshment in one of the fine cafés on the square outside.

RESTAURANTS

€€ **Antico Fattore**, Via Lambertesca 1/3r, *T* 055 288 975; closed Sunday and late July–early August. Flawlessly prepared dishes from the Tuscan tradition.

Osteria del Porcellino, Via Val di Lamona 7r, *T* 055 264 148; always open. Good, simple, hearty Tuscan cooking.

Ottorino, Via delle Oche 12-16r, *T* 055 215 151; closed Sunday. Delicious Tuscan pastas and meats; unfortunately it's been discovered by tour groups.

Paoli, Via dei Tavolini 12r, *T* 055 216 215; closed Tuesday and in August. The Gothic Revival interiors of this favourite of Florentines go hand-in-hand with a scrupulous regard for tradition in the kitchen.

€€€ **Hotel Bristol**, Via dei Pescioni 2, *T* 055 287 814. This elegant restaurant in a luxury hotel is justly famous for its delicious and imaginative seasonal Tuscan cuisine.

Oliviero, Via delle Terme 1r, *T* 055 212 421; closed Sunday and in August. Creative interpretations of traditional recipes, coupled with classic Florentine ambience, are the hallmarks of this venerable establishment.

WINE BARS

€ **Cantinetta dei Verrazzano**, Via de' Tavolini 18-20, *T* 055 268 590; closed Sunday. Simply the best wine bar in downtown Florence, serving a wide variety of sweet and savoury baked goods, focaccia-bread sandwiches, *cecina* (a chick-pea pancake), and delicious wines from the Chianti estate of Giovanni da Verrazzano, the gentleman who discovered New York harbour.

Coquinarius, Via delle Oche 15r, *T* 055 230 2153; closed Sunday. A lovely little place in the back streets right by the duomo, with great wines and a constantly changing selection of Tuscan delicacies.

Enoteca de' Giraldi, Via de' Giraldi 4r, *T* 055 216 518; closed Sunday and holidays. A little hard to find (Via de' Giraldi is a cross-street of Via Pandolfini and Borgo degli Albizi), this pleasant place specializes in lesser-known Tuscan wines, excellent salads and delicious cheeses.

Quasigratis, Via de' Castellani 25r, *T* 055 264 128, closed Sunday and in January. An old-fashioned *vinaio* where you eat *salame* sandwiches and hard-boiled eggs standing up and drink out of *rasini*, little glasses filled to the brim with simple red wine.

Vini, Via de' Cimatori, *T* 055 239 6096, closed Sunday. Another simple, traditional place; a tight squeeze at lunch time.

CAFÉS

€ **Astor Caffè**, Piazza Duomo 20r. Strategically situated opposite the north flank of the cathedral, with live music at night.

Caffè Italiano, Via Condotta 12. Good light meals and desserts, near Piazza della Signoria.

Gilli, Piazza della Repubblica 39r. One of Florence's most classical cafés, with beautiful antique interiors and summer seating on the Piazza della Repubblica.

Giubbe Rosse, Piazza della Repubblica 13-14r. Once a place of poets and painters (De Chirico hung out here), with fair-weather seating on the Piazza della Repubblica.

Hotel Savoy, Piazza della Repubblica 7. Good for people watching over a light lunch or at the cocktail hour; outdoor seating in summer.

Paszkowski, Piazza della Repubblica 6. Another elegant café on Florence's central square, with live music on summer evenings.

Perché No?, Via dei Tavolini 19r. The best ice cream in town; the crème caramel is especially famous, though the chocolate is also memorable.

Rivoire, Piazza della Signoria 5r. The world's most sinful hot chocolate (try it with whipped cream!) plus pastries and pralines to die for; fair-weather seating on the piazza.

shopping

Because of the immense numbers of people who visit Florence each year, the city has more than its fair share of sophisticated shops. Most of these line the streets between the duomo and the Arno, in the city centre - and the neighbouring Via dei Tornabuoni and Via della Vigna Nuova, which are listed in the section of this guide devoted to Santa Maria Novella and its neighbourhood.

ACCESSORIES

Bally, Via Calimala 11. Switzerland's finest ultrachic luxury brand: footwear, luggage, handbags and ready-to-wear.

Borsalino, Via Por la Russa 40. Classic men's hats.

Coccinelle, Via Por Santa Maria 49. Italy's affordable accessories brand offers every kind of tote bag, shopper or purse imaginable, plus snazzy leather goods.

Furla, Via dei Calzaiuoli 47. One of the more venerable Italian leather-goods and accessories labels, now also making handcrafted women's footwear.

Gucci, Via Roma 32. The famous leather designer's accessories store, arranged on three floors and offering everything imaginable *pour femme, homme* and - yes - *chien/chat*.

Mandarina Duck, Via Por Santa Maria 23r. Everything you could dream of from this trendy maker of travel bags and cases, briefcases, purses and multi-functional bags.

BOOKS

Edison, Piazza Repubblica 5. Books in Italian, English, French, German, Spanish and Russian, plus sofas and a coffee bar.

Libreria del Porcellino, Piazza Mercato Nuovo 6r. Beautiful coffee-table books and travel publications, and lots of old wood.

CLOTHES

Basic, Via Porta Rossa 109-115. A good all-around women's ready-to-wear store, with international brands including Alberta Feretti Philosophy casuals and Faliero Sarti knitwear.

Boston Tailor, Via Vecchietti 17. Elegant suits and handcrafted accessories for men only.

Bottega delle Antiche Terme, Borgo Santissimi Apostoli 16. Men's shirts and trousers made to measure in a shop that was once a spa; over 500 fabrics to choose from, in cotton, silk and linen.

Brioni, Via Calimala 22. Men's suits magnificently cut from the best English and Italian fabrics.

Coin, Via Calzaiuoli 56. Italy's top of the range department store, occupying a 16c palazzo in the heart of the city.

Del Moro Cappelli, Via Sant'Elisabetta 15. Hats for all occasions, each handmade or custom tailored; also, a selection of brand-name ready-to-wear hats.

Diesel, Via dei Lamberti 13. Hip, cult fashion store on two levels, with 'signature' denims on the ground floor and complete womenswear and accessories collections on the floor above.

Emporio Armani, Piazza Strozzi 16. Armani's high-quality fabrics and tailoring, in styles that are sportier and younger than those of the flagship line; men and women's apparel plus accessories, eyewear, perfume, etc.

Guess, Via degli Speziali 9-11. The LA womenswear label offers everything from jeans to backless evening dresses and strappy shoes and sandals to match.

Hugo Boss, Piazza della Repubblica 46. Germany's trendy clothing maker makes apparel for women as well as men, but only the menswear is sold here - the Boss label, known for its bold contemporary designs and quality detailing, plus the sportier Black, Orange and Red lines.

La Rinascente, Piazza della Repubblica 1. Italy's premier department store, with an especially good housewares section featuring Alessi and other designer names.

L'Essentiel, Via del Corso 10r. Beautiful and original women's ready-to-wear fashions.

Luisa, Via Roma 19-21. All the hottest labels for men and women are here, and a good bit of less sizzling stuff too; the only place in town where you can put pieces by Yves Saint Laurent and Juicy Couture in the same bag.

Max & Co, Via dei Calzaiuoli 89. MaxMara's youngest label, with smooth trendy women's clothing and a good range of shoes, handbags and silk scarfs.

MaxMara, Via dei Pecori 23. Max Mara's famous camel-hair coats, accompanied by the whole family of MaxMara brands - Sportmax, Sportmix Code, Weekend and MaxMara Basic - and by a wide range of accessories, from shoes to handbags to silk scarfs.

Miss Sixty, Via Roma 20. Small but jam-packed with embroidered, sprayed and studded denim jeans and jackets, plus girl stuff like bags, belts and sunglasses.

Miu Miu, Via Roma 8. Miu Miu is Miuccia Prada and what you see started as her experimental collection in 1992 - men's and women's clothes and accessories, colourful and edgy.

Moda Sartoriale, Via del Purgatorio 22. Capable men's tailors with a faithful following of rock stars and heads of government - and quite rightly, as it's difficult to imagine a more superb suit.

Murphy & Nye, Via Calimala 16-18. Sailmakers Jim Murphy and Harry Nye Jr and their heirs have been working with fabrics since 1933; their sturdy yet fashionable clothing for men, women and children is sold over a counter shaped like a sailing boat.

Patrizia Pepe, Piazza San Giovanni 12. Pepe is 'pepper' and the clothes in this store are certainly hot - thanks to the creative verve of Tuscan entrepreneurs Patrizia Bambi and Claudio Orrea; very popular with Italian women, the goods range from snug tailored suits to floaty evening dresses, encompassing also a wide range of accessories.

Piero Guidi, Via Calimala 12. The colourful leather-and-fabric creations of this unconventional designer are popular with young men and women from Japan with a penchant for the experimental.

Prenatal, Via Brunelleschi 22. Just about everything for young children, babies and mums-to-be, from clothes to prams to toys, games and books.

Replay, Via Por Santa Maria 27. A favourite of young Italians on the lookout for stylish jeans, denim and casual fashions; also a colourful children's collection.

Strenesse, Via Porta Rossa 81-85. If you like Armani you might look at Gabriele Strehle's creations for Strenesse; the Florentine store of this German maker of upscale womenswear (and recently, menswear) plays to the same crowd.

THE HOME

Coin, Via Calzaiuoli 56. Italy's high quality department store has the best of everything - including location, occupying a 16c palazzo in the heart of the city.

La Rinascente, Piazza della Repubblica 1. Italy's premier department store, with an especially good housewares section featuring Alessi and other designer names.

Marchi, Borgo degli Albizi 71r. Fine fabrics and home furnishings.

JEWELLERY

Blue Point, Via Calzaiuoli 39r. Silver and gold earrings, necklaces, bracelets especially popular with teens.

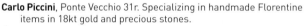

Carlo Piccini, Ponte Vecchio 31r. Specializing in handmade Florentine items in 18kt gold and precious stones.

Cassetti, Ponte Vecchio 52. Gold jewellery and watches, especially Bulgari and Audemars Piguet.

Marchi, Ponte Vecchio 44-48. Wide range of 18kt gold, sterling silver, diamonds and precious stones.

KIDS

Baroni, Via Porta Rossa 56. Everything your kids might need, from clothes (le Petit Bateau skirts and tops, Oshkosh denims, and Baroni's own line of dresses made from Liberty fabrics) to linens and blankets - all made of hand-finished natural fabrics - and clothes for mothers-to-be.

Benetton 0-12, Via dei Cerretani 60-22. Trendy clothing and accessories for the little ones, and a colourful, stylish range of maternity wear.

Città del Sole, Via dei Cimatori 21r. The best place to go for educational toys.

Coin, Via Calzaiuoli 56. Italy's top of the range department store has apparel for all ages.

Disney Store, Via Calzaiuoli 69r. If Walt and his crew created it, it's here.

Natura e..., Via dello Studio 30r. Kids of all ages can (and do) spend hours just browsing in this science shop.

Prenatal, Via Brunelleschi 22. Just about everything for young children, babies and mums-to-be, from clothes to prams to toys, games and books.

LINGERIE

Calzedonia, Via dei Calzaiuoli 99r. Sexy and affordable lingerie, hosiery and underthings.

Intimissimi, Via Calzaiuoli 99r. Lots of silky, lacy things, none of which can be worn out of the house.

MUSIC

Ricordi, Via Brunelleschi. Italy's music megastore has every classical/jazz/rock/folk/world recording ever made, anywhere – and if it's not in stock, they'll get it fast.

SHOES

Calvani, Via degli Speziali 7. Italy's most piquant avant-garde shoe designs.

Camper, Via Por Santa Maria 47. Fun, unconventional shoes for men and women.

Fausto Santini, Via dei Calzaiuoli 95. Singular designs for men and women by Rome's most brilliant shoe and handbag maker.

Fratelli Rossetti, Piazza della Repubblica 43-45. Always one for innovation, Rossetti's men's and women's footwear is diverse, the details rich and the technique and materials perfect.

Italobalestri, Piazza Santa Maria Maggiore 7. Exotic couture shoes for women and a more sober collection of polished leather lace-ups for men.

Nannini, Via Porta Rossa 64. Shoes for men and women, beautifully crafted from the softest leathers; handbags, travel cases and eyewear share the same standard of excellence.

Paola del Lungo, Via Porta Rossa 7. Men's and women's shoes and accessories with unusual fabrics and original design ideas.

Pollini, Via Calimala 12. Quality is the hallmark of this Italian footwear specialist, who also produces ready-to-wear lines for the major European designers.

Raspini, Via Por Santa Maria 72. Florence's most famous name in footware, plus the best of Italian ready-to-wear apparel for men and women.

Sergio Rossi, Via Roma 15. Seriously sexy shoes (for men and women), from one of Italy's leading designers; also bags and small leather goods.

SPORT

Champion, Via Por Santa Maria 52-54. Casual styles as well as serious technical gear from the American sportswear specialist.

Footlocker, Via dei Calzaiuoli 27-35. Brand-name trainers plus cool urban- and sportswear from Italian houses Fila, Lotto and Umbro.

Murphy & Nye, Via Calimala 16-18. Sailmakers Jim Murphy and Harry Nye Jr and their heirs have been working with fabrics since 1933; their sturdy yet fashionable clothing for men, women and children is sold over a counter shaped like a sailing boat.

Universo Sport, Piazza Duomo 6. Two floors of the finest sportswear, accessories and sports equipment, for grownups and kids alike.

STATIONERY

Il Papiro, Lungarno Acciaiuoli 42r, Piazza Duomo 24r and Via dei Tavolini 13r. Florence's leading handmade paper shop, selling beautiful stationery, giftwrap, bound notebooks, cards, and more.

Pineider, Piazza della Signoria 13r. Florence's finest stationery and writing accessories.

Palazzo Pitti and the Boboli Gardens

OPEN	**Galleria Palatina & Appartamenti Reali**, Tues-Sun 8.15-18.50. **Museo degli Argenti**, Tues-Sun 8.15-13.50; 2nd and 4th Mon 8.15-13.50 **Galleria d'Arte Moderna & Galleria del Costume**, Tues-Sat 8.15-13.50; 1st, 3rd, 5th Sun 8.15-13.50; 2nd, 4th Mon 8.15-13.50 **Giardino di Boboli**, Nov-Feb 8.15-16.30; March 8.15-17.30; April, May, Sept, Oct 8.15-18.30; June-Aug 8.15-19.30 **Museo delle Porcellane**, Mon-Sat 8.30-13.50; 1st, 3rd, 5th Sun 8.30-13.50; 2nd, 4th Mon 8.30-13.50
CLOSED	**Galleria Palatina & Appartamenti Reali**, Mon **Museo degli Argenti**, 2nd and 4th Sun, 1st 3rd and 5th Mon **Galleria d'Arte Moderna & Galleria del Costume**, 2nd, 4th Sun; 1st, 3rd, 5th Mon **Giardino di Boboli**, 1st and last Mon **Museo delle Porcellane**, 2nd, 4th Sun; 1st, 3rd, 5th Mon
CHARGES	**Galleria Palatina & Appartamenti Reali**, full price €6.50, booking (optional) €1.55 **Museo degli Argenti**, full price €2.00; booking (optional) €1.55 **Museo degli Argenti & Giardino di Boboli**, full price €3.00, reduced price €1.50 **Galleria d'Arte Moderna & Galleria del Costume**, full price €5.00; booking (optional) €1.55 **Giardino di Boboli**, full price €2.00, booking (optional): €1.55 **Giardino di Boboli & Museo degli Argenti**, full price €3.00, reduced price €1.50 **Museo delle Porcellane**, included in Boboli ticket Ticket sales end 45 minutes before closing An **inclusive ticket** gives admission to the Galleria Palatina, Museo degli Argenti, the Galleria d'Arte Moderna and the Giardino di Boboli: full price €10.50, reduced price €5.25; with entry to the Galleria Palatina after 16.00: full price €8.00, reduced price €4.00 The inclusive ticket is **not available** when exhibitions are being held in any of the museums All Pitti museums offer a 50% reduction for 18-25-year-olds from the EU and for accredited teachers Admission is free for young people under 18, school groups (participants must be listed on school letterhead), accredited journalists, those accompanying the disabled and EU citizens over 60

TELEPHONE	Galleria Palatina & Appartamenti Reali, 055 238 8614
	Museo degli Argenti, 055 238 8709
	Galleria d'Arte Moderna, 055 238 8601
	Galleria del Costume, 055 238 8713
	Giardino di Boboli, 055 210 741
	Museo delle Porcellane, 055 238 8605
WWW.	firenzemusei.it
MAIN ENTRANCE	Piazza Pitti 1
DISABLED ACCESS	To all museums and galleries (ask at Reception)
GUIDED VISITS	Can be organized by contacting the Education Department of the Curator's Office (T 055 238 8658), or the booking service (T 055 294 883) Audio tours available
SERVICES	Palazzo Pitti. Cloakroom and café off the ground floor courtyard, south side. Museum shop at Galleria Palatina & Appartamenti Reali, first floor
	Boboli Gardens. Café in Kaffeehaus except in mid-winter

The massive Pitti Palace on Florence's left bank, the Oltrarno, was built for the Florentine banker Luca Pitti after 1457 and is supposedly based on a design by Filippo Brunelleschi. The original building, just two storeys with seven windows overlooking the piazza, took some 400 years to acquire its present appearance.

Its long history as the palace of the ruling dynasties of Florence began with its acquisition by Cosimo I, later Grand Duke of Tuscany, in the middle of the 16c. He commissioned Bartolomeo Ammannati (1558-70) to construct two wings at the back of the building, forming the magnificent courtyard that leads on to the slopes of the Boboli hill. At the same time, the land behind the palace was gradually transformed into the Boboli Gardens.

For 300 years, from the second half of the 16c until 1859, when the Grand Duchy of Tuscany was annexed to the Kingdom of Italy, the palace and its courtyard were the focus for dazzling public and dynastic events and celebrations. Here were held the weddings, baptisms, and funerals of the Medici and Hapsburg-Lorraine, who succeeded the Medici as rulers of Tuscany in 1736. And here the lords of Florence accumulated the collections that make the Galleria Palatina so important today: Cardinal Leopoldo de' Medici acquiring mainly Venetian paintings, and Grand Prince

Palazzo Pitti

Ferdinando, the son of Grand Duke Cosimo III de' Medici, contributing an exceptional group of Renaissance and Baroque paintings. The Hapsburg-Lorraines arranged the collections on the first floor of the palace, and their manner of hanging the works has been preserved to the present day. They also added rooms and paintings that accorded with Neoclassical tastes.

Officially opened to the public in 1828, under the House of Savoy, the palace was further enlarged and the number of works on display was doubled.

HIGHLIGHTS

Old-master paintings	Galleria Palatina
Post-Impressionist paintings	Galleria d'Arte Moderna
Renaissance women's fashions	Galleria del Costume
Frescoed halls, antiques and jewellery	Museo degli Argenti

GALLERIA PALATINA AND APPARTAMENTI REALI

One of the more distinctive features of the Galleria Palatina is the arrangement of the paintings, densely packed to form a pleasing display of size and colour in harmony with the ceiling decorations, furniture and sculpture. Each room has a particular character and each takes its name from the scene frescoed on the ceiling; the decoration begun under the Medici and continued by the Lorraines until well into the 19c. The Lorraines were largely responsible for supplying the rooms with furniture produced by the Opificio delle Pietre Dure, the famous manufacturer of Florentine mosaic work in precious and semi-precious stones, and with the precious objects that lend the gallery its characteristic opulence.

The Galleria Palatina occupies the most important rooms on the first floor: six rooms overlooking the piazza and those in the north wing at the rear of the building, previously the winter apartments of the Medici Grand Dukes. From the entrance foyer visitors are directed briefly through the Appartamenti Reali, which occupy rooms I-XX on the west side of the palace front and overlooking the Boboli Gardens.

The Royal Apartments
In the second half of the 17c these chambers were the rooms reserved for the Medici Grand Prince Ferdinando (1665-1713) who died before he could accede to the throne. He decorated his apartments with an impressive collection of some thousand paintings, later incorporated into the collections of the Galleria Palatina and the Uffizi. The apartments were enlarged, redecorated and refurnished, most notably after the Restoration (1814) to suit the taste of the successors to the Medici, the Grand Dukes of the House of Lorraine. In 1853 the walls of the first five rooms were covered with sumptuous silk brocade and the floors with French carpets. With the advent of the Savoy the Pitti became for a brief period the official residence of the ruling family of the newly united Kingdom of Italy. In the 1880s furniture, paintings and other precious objects – including an important group of portraits of the French royal family at the time of Louis XV - were brought from the Ducal Palace in Parma.

The Palatine Collection is entered from the Anticamera degli Staffieri (1). Here circulation is directed through a number of 'lesser rooms' leading to the six great rooms (23-8), overlooking Piazza Pitti, that contain the masterpieces of the collection. Just slightly less opulent than the great reception halls, these minor rooms contain **antique sculpture** from the Villa Medici in Rome (in Room 2), and several fine **paintings**: Filippo Lippi's 1450 *Virgin and Child with Scenes from the Life of St Anne*, Botticelli's 1470 *Portrait of a Young Man* and Pontormo's *Adoration of the Magi* of 1520 (Room 14); Titian's *Portrait of a Man* of 1520-30 (Room 16); Perugino's *Mary Magdalene* of 1496-1500 (Room 17); Raphael's *Madonna and Child, St John the Baptist and Saints* ('*Madonna* dell'Impannata'), painted around 1514, and Andrea del Sarto's *Madonna and Child with Saints* ('*Pala di Gambassi*') of 1525-6 (Room 19), and last but not least, Caravaggio's *Sleeping Cupid* of 1608 (Room 21).

The superb Empire bathroom was designed by Giuseppe Cacialli for Elisa Baciocchi, Grand Duchess of Tuscany and sister of Napoleon Bonaparte, between 1808 and 1813. She intended the adjacent Sala dell'Educazione di Giove (Room 21) as a bedroom for her brother, but Napoleon never stayed here. The adjacent Stove Room (Room 22, Sala della Stufa) once housed the heating pipes to warm this and the other bedrooms.

SALA DELL'ILIADE *Room 23* This room has scenes from Mount Olympus on the ceiling and episodes from Homer's *Iliad* in the lunettes, painted by Luigi Sabatelli (1819-25). Here is **Artemesia Gentileschi**'s famous *Judith*, dated 1614-20 - a powerful, dramatic picture with an ingenious composition: the two women stand in the twisted pose known as *contrapposto*, forming perfect mirror-images of one another. The highly original work had a profound influence on Florentine painting of its period.

Justus Sustermans was the Medici's official painter from his arrival in Florence from Flanders in 1619 until his death some 60 years later. A friend of Rubens, he was also a diligent student of Van Dyck and Velázquez, as the lively portraits of *Waldemar Christian, Prince of Denmark* and *Mattias de' Medici, Governor of Siena* (1660) show.

Andrea del Sarto's monumental *Assumption of the Virgin* ('*Assunta Panciatichi*') was painted in 1522-3 for the Florentine businessman Bartolomeo Panciatichi. Its revolutionary composition, with the division of the episode on two levels and strongly contrasting, shot colours, had a lasting impact on 16c and 17c painting. Andrea adopted the same composition in his 1526 altarpiece of the subject for the Passerini family in Cortona, positioned opposite the earlier painting.

Raphael's dignified portrait of a pregnant woman, *Portrait of a Woman Expecting a Child* ('*La Gravida*') is one made by the young painter around 1507, during his last period in Florence. The bold

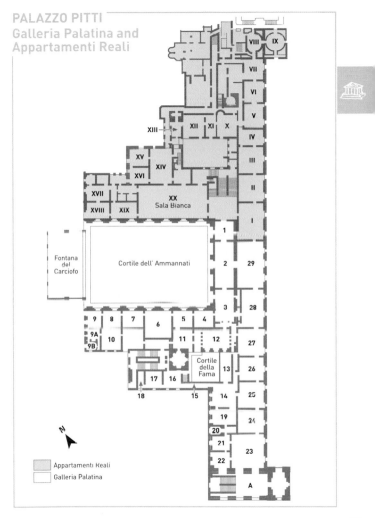

PALAZZO PITTI
Galleria Palatina and
Appartamenti Reali

VIII IX

VII

VI

V

XIII XII XI X

IV

XV III
XIV

XVI II

XVII

XVIII XIX I

XX
Sala Bianca

1

Fontana
del
Carciofo

Cortile dell' Ammannati

2 29

3 28

9 8 7 6 5 4

9A
9B 10 11 12 27

Cortile
della
Fama 13 26

17 16

18 15 14 25

19 24

20

21 23

22

N

Appartamenti Reali
Galleria Palatina

A

colouring of the woman's garments against the dark background
and the formal complexity of the painting distinguish it from those
Raphael did during his first Roman period. Raphael's Florentine
portraits clearly influenced **Ridolfo del Ghirlandaio,** the gifted son
of the more famous Domenico Ghirlandaio, whose *Portrait of a
Woman* was painted in 1508.

SALA DI SATURNO *Room 24* The frescoes and stucco in this
opulent room were created between 1663 and 1665 by Ciro Ferri, a
pupil of Pietro da Cortona who here followed his master's designs.
They show Prince Ferdinando, in the guise of Hercules, ascending
Mount Olympus to be greeted by the gods; the four lunettes
represent scenes from the lives of eminent Greeks and Romans
(Scipio, Lycurgus, Sulla and Syrus).

Here are no fewer than seven paintings by **Raphael**. The
Madonna del Granduca (c 1506) is the simplest and most moving of
Raphael's portrayals of the Virgin and Child: the soft modelling of
the figures against the dark background recalls Leonardo's use of
light and shadow, whereas the precise drawing and 'geometric'
conception of form denote a debt to the painter's master,
Perugino. An original touch of Raphael's is the elimination of the
landscape background traditional in treatments of this theme.

The double portraits of **Agnolo** and **Maddalena Doni** (1505-6) show
the people who paid for Michelangelo's Uffizi **Doni Tondo** (and
many other works of Florentine Renaissance art). The portraits
may have formed a diptych like Piero della Francesca's portrayal
of the Duke and Duchess of Urbino (in the Uffizi). Maddalena's
pose recalls that of Leonardo's **Mona Lisa** (Louvre, Paris). The
close attention to detail, especially of dress and jewellery, is
characteristic of Flemish painting and may have reached
Raphael through the work of Hans Memling.

The *Vision of Ezekiel* (c 1518) shows the energy and imagination,
and the complex balance of form, light and colour that Raphael
applied in his later works to create a naturalistic cosmic vision.

The most famous of Raphael's Madonnas is the *Madonna and
Child with St John the Baptist* of c 1516, known as the '*Madonna della
Seggiola*'. It belongs to the artist's late period in Rome and is his

only *tondo*, reviving the circular composition popular in Florence in the Quattrocento. Raphael's inspiration was the work of Donatello, showing Mother and Child in a close embrace, which had already attracted him during his Florentine period. In this composition the intertwined forms create a more complex rhythm, more monumental and underscored by full, glowing, almost Venetian colouring. The original frame is by Giovanni Battista Foggini.

Perugino's *Lamentation* (1495) was painted for the convent of the Poor Clares in Florence and is typical of the controlled lyricism of his compositions. Perugino, influenced at an early age by Piero della Francesca, introduced the Umbrian style to Florence when he continued his training in Verrocchio's workshop.

SALA DI GIOVE *Room 25* Once the throne room of the Grand Dukes, this gold-and-white hall was decorated with stucco and frescoes by Pietro da Cortona between 1642 and 1644. Among the masterpieces by Andrea del Sarto, Giovanni Lanfranco and Fra' Bartolomeo, the stars on this stage are **Raphael**'s *Portrait of a Young Woman* ('*La Velata*', c 1513) and **Giorgione**'s *Three Ages of Man* (c 1500).

In this portrait of an unknown veiled woman Raphael breaks away from the influences of Leonardo and Perugino, visible in other female portraits. From the sculptural feel of those pictures he arrives at a freer, more luminous technique that can only be explained as the result of a new mastery of painting acquired while working on the frescoes in the Vatican Stanze. The loveliness of the face framed by the veil is matched by the bravura 'set piece' of the ruched silken sleeve, an inimitable pictorial tour de force. The intensity of the sitter's gaze and the beauty of her face linger in the memory as peaks of formal perfection.

The allegorical significance of the *Three Ages of Man* is now rejected and the painting is seen rather as a singing lesson or 'concert of voices' typical of the musical Venetian culture to which Giorgione belonged. The attribution to Giorgione is fairly recent; the modern consensus is that this is a work of the artist's youth, strongly reminiscent of both Bellini and Leonardo, but already rich in motifs that the artist would develop in later years.

SALA DI MARTE *Room 26* Pietro da Cortona painted the ceiling with an *Allegory of War and Peace* surrounding a triumphal vision of the Medici coat of arms, between 1644 and 1646.

Not to be missed in this room are two masterpieces by **Pieter Paul Rubens**. Rubens painted *The Four Philosophers* around 1611-2, in memory of his brother Philip, a pupil of the philosopher Justus Lipsius, who is also shown. Both men had recently died. The artist portrayed himself at the upper left, and at the lower right he added Jan van de Wouvere, a fellow student of Philip's. The four tulips beside the bust of Seneca symbolize the lives of the four sitters (two have already opened out). The books lying on the carpet-covered table, the view of the Palatine Hill in the background, the gestures and the intensity of the glances make this group portrait a masterpiece of 17c art.

In *The Consequences of War* (1637-8) the allegorical title obscures the painting's true subject: on the left Europe, dressed in black, casts her hands upwards before the open-doored temple of Janus, while in the centre naked Venus endeavours to restrain Mars, who grasps a shield and a drawn sword as he strides into battle dragged by the Furies. In his march he tramples on books and overturns the Arts, as well as a young woman with a baby at her breast. Sending this painting in 1638 to his colleague Justus Sustermans, court painter to the Medici, Rubens explained its meaning in relation to the Thirty Years War, which was raging in his homeland.

Here are also several fine Renaissance portraits. *Ippolito de' Medici*, son of Giuliano Duke of Nemours, was created cardinal at the age of 18 by Clement VII. More interested in war than in a career in the Church, he had himself painted by **Titian** when he was in Bologna in 1535, dressed in the Hungarian style in memory of his role in repelling the siege of Vienna by the Turks. The harmony of violet and magenta emphasize the martial bearing and somewhat cruel expression of the young warrior.

Anthony van Dyck's extraordinary symphony of red - the colour of the cardinalate - was meant to celebrate the elevation of *Guido Bentivoglio* to the Sacred College. His portrait (c 1625) is the concluding masterpiece of the Italian period of the greatest genius among Rubens' pupils. The full-length, life-sized figure dominates its surroundings with the nobility of its lineaments, the elegance of the hands, the refinement of the clothing. The cardinal emerges from the background with a majestic presence, subtly controlled by acute psychological insight.

Alvise Cornaro (1475-1566), an aristocratic man of letters, spent his life in Padua, the centre of university studies, where he protected scientists and scholars and wrote a number of treatises. Rather than emphasize his sitter's versatility, **Tintoretto** in this portrait of c 1560-5 concentrates on his very human aspect, through a sombre harmony of greys and blacks.

SALA DI APOLLO *Room 27* The decoration of this room was begun by Pietro da Cortona in 1646 and completed by Ciro Ferri in 1661, following the master's design.

Titian's *Mary Magdalene* (c 1555) was painted for the court of Urbino around 1555. The model's voluptuous physical beauty is barely concealed by her lavish waves of auburn hair. Titian's superb command of colour and free, confident brushwork are here at their best.

Despite the title, nothing is known about the identity of the sitter in the *Portrait of a Gentleman* ('*The Grey-Eyed Nobleman*' or '*Englishman*'), painted around 1545. Presumably he was of high social standing, as appears from the sober suit, the heavy gold chain, the gloves held in the right hand and the faintly haughty expression. The portrait, painted at the height of Titian's career, is a subtle analysis of the sitter's personality and a symphony of greys and blacks, tones that give the youthful face weight and authority.

Andrea del Sarto's *Lamentation over the Dead Christ* ('*Pietà di Luco*'), painted in 1523-4, has a sense of monumentality reminiscent of Michelangelo and Raphael, while the bright, transparent colours, boldly juxtaposed, foreshadow the achievements of the Mannerist painters Pontormo and Rosso Fiorentino.

The *Madonna and Child with St Elizabeth and St John the Baptist* ('*Sacra Famiglia Medici*'), painted for Ottaviano de' Medici in 1529, is one of Andrea's private devotional works. The artist learned the *sfumato* shading effects from Leonardo, the clarity of the design and the sculptural quality of the figures from Michelangelo, and the clever composition from Raphael - especially from the Holy Families of his Florentine period. The combination of these influences, fused with Andrea del Sarto's particular solemnity, results in a highly original and appealing style.

SALA DI VENERE *Room 28* Antonio Canova's *Venus* (*'Venere Italica'*, 1810) reflects the great Neoclassical sculptor's 'modern' interpretation of ancient Greek aesthetic values. The smooth surface finish of the marble body and the folds of the drapery denote a technical ability that had not been equalled since the time of Bernini - some 200 years earlier. Canova's *Venus* was offered to Napoleon in exchange for the *Venus dei Medici*, which he had taken from the Tribune of the Uffizi (returned in 1816).

   Pieter Paul Rubens' *Peasants Returning from the Fields* (1640), and the companion piece showing *Ulysses on the Island of the Phaeacians*, in the same room, are delightful images of the natural world with peasants, animals and trees bathed in the warm glow of the setting sun.

   Harbour at Sunset, a large canvas (c 1645) by the Neapolitan **Salvator Rosa**, and the companion work depicting a *Harbour with a Lighthouse* were painted during the artist's Florentine period, 1640-9. In *Harbour at Sunset* a sense of depth is created by the soft light of the setting sun, as in the work of Claude Lorrain. Rosa had a considerable impact on the development of landscape painting in the 17c and 18c.

   Cardinal Leopoldo de' Medici, an enthusiastic collector of Venetian painting, bought *The Concert* (1510-2) in Venice in 1654 as a work by **Giorgione**. Today some scholars believe it is an early work by his pupil, Titian, though others suspect that more than one hand was involved. In both its style and its poetical subject matter the painting is still strongly reminiscent of Giorgione, whose paintings represent a slightly unreal world in which the figures appear spiritually remote.

   The informal title of **Titian**'s 1536 *Portrait of a Young Woman*,

'La Bella', can hardly be disputed, although the identity of this beautiful dark-eyed woman is still open to debate. Dressed in a gold-embroidered blue gown and wearing conspicuous jewellery, she is sometimes identified with Francesco Maria della Rovere, the Duke of Urbino's lover and probably Titian's model for the *Venus of Urbino* (Uffizi).

Titian's **Portrait of Pietro Aretino** (c 1545) marks the friendship between the painter and the celebrated man of letters and satirist - a friendship that failed to survive the painting's completion. Aretino detested it and accused Titian of working in haste, misunderstanding Titian's painterly technique, which became increasingly impressionistic in his later years. The writer therefore sent it to the first Grand Duke, Cosimo I, asking for a substantial payment in return.

The exit from the gallery is through the Sala delle Nicchie, named after the six niches - there were originally ten - housing Roman copies of Greek sculpture, first displayed here at the end of the 16c.

GALLERY OF MODERN ART

Located on the top floor of the Pitti Palace with splendid views of the Boboli Gardens, the Gallery of Modern Art was established in 1914 and opened to the public in 1924. Many of its 30 rooms were decorated in the 19c under the last grand dukes of the Lorraine dynasty, Ferdinando III and Leopoldo II. The collection includes over 2000 works providing an overview of Tuscan painting from the 18c to 20c, and a small number of paintings from other Italian and foreign schools.

The Gallery also possesses an important collection of works by the Tuscan Post-Impressionists known as the **Macchiaioli**: Silvestro Lega (*Il Canto dello Stornello*), Giovanni Fattori (**Lo Staffato**, **La Battaglia di Custoza**), and Raffaello Sernesi (**Colli Fiorentini**). 20c painting is represented by Gino Severini, Ardengo Soffici, Giorgio De Chirico, Felice Casorati and Ottone Rosai.

COSTUME GALLERY

Opened in 1983, the Costume Gallery is housed in the Palazzina della Meridiana, begun by Gaspare Paoletti in 1776 and completed by Pasquale Poccianti during the Grand Duchy of Leopoldo II. It houses a large collection of antique period costumes. The 13 rooms describe the evolution of fashion and clothing, with particular attention to women's costumes from rigid 18c corsets to short dresses of the 1960s.

MUSEO DEGLI ARGENTI

Housed in the magnificently frescoed summer apartments of the grand dukes, the Museo degli Argenti displays the treasures in silver, ivory and precious stones, and other curiosities collected by the Medici and Lorraine. On the ground floor, the **Sala di Luca Pitti** takes its name from a polychrome terracotta bust of the palace's first owner, which is displayed in the company of seven busts of the Medici and painted portraits of members of Florence's ruling dynasty by Sustermans.

The **Sala di Giovanni di San Giovanni** is the largest and most sumptuously decorated room. It is named after the artist who painted the large, colourful frescoes on the walls and ceiling for the wedding of Ferdinando II and Vittoria della Rovere in 1635. The bride and groom are depicted in the large vault composition. On the walls are scenes exalting the glory of Lorenzo il Magnifico.

The **Sala Buia** (left) holds the extraordinary collection of antique Roman, Byzantine, and Venetian vases in semi-precious stone assembled by Lorenzo il Magnifico. Many of these bear Lorenzo's monogram, 'LA.V.R.MED', set by Florentine goldsmiths. The adjacent Grotticina, has a fine *pietra dura* and marble floor, 17c vault frescoes with birds, and a beautiful basin, possibly dating from the 16c, in front of the window.

Beyond the Sala di Giovanni di San Giovanni are three state rooms with marvellous trompe l'oeil frescoes (1635-41) by Angelo Michele Colonna and Agostino Mitelli showing architectural perspectives interspersed with scenes of history, myth and allegory.

The **Camera del Granduca Gian Gastone** has splendid displays of amber and ivory, some in gilded wood cabinets. The mezzanine floor, reached by a delightful little staircase, is home to the stunning Medici **jewellery collection**; especially beautiful are the pieces that belonged to the Electress Anna Maria, last of the Medici, and those from the treasury of Ferdinando III. There is also a lovely loggia with Mexican vases, and rooms of rare and exotic objects from distant lands.

THE BOBOLI GARDENS

On the hillside behind the palace lie the magnificent Boboli Gardens, 45 hectares (111 acres) of Baroque landscaping laid out for Cosimo I de' Medici and his wife Eleonora di Toledo as a setting for pageants and court entertainments.

The gardens were begun in 1550 by **Tribolo** (Niccolò di Raffaello de' Pericoli) and continued, over two centuries, by **Davide Fortini, Giorgio Vasari, Bartolomeo Ammannati, Bernardo Buontalenti** and **Giulio** and **Alfonso Parigi**.

Opened to the public for the first time in 1766, they comprise two loosely defined areas: the upper gardens near the palace, laid out along a north-south axis, and the lower gardens to the south, developing east to west. The former is the ceremonial area, with structures specifically designed for pageants and spectacles. The latter are a living metaphor for the pursuit of knowledge through reason and intuition, with a broad, straight avenue lined by majestic cypresses and Classical statuary (the way of reason) and a system of meandering footpaths through dark woods of ilex and laurel (the way of intuition) both leading to an elliptical fountain (knowledge). Many of the 170 statues that adorn the gardens are restored Roman works; others are the work of 16c and 17c artists (Baccio Bandinelli, Vincenzo de' Rossi, Giambologna and others) and some have yet to be identified.

There are four entrances: from the courtyard of Palazzo Pitti, the Via Romana, the Porta Romana, and the Forte di Belvedere, at the top of the hill; usually only the first two are open to visitors. The main exit is through the north wing of Palazzo Pitti, though you can also leave by the Via Romana and Porta Romana gates.

The entrance from Ammannati's great Mannerist courtyard of Palazzo Pitti leads directly to the upper garden, passing on the way the *Fontana del Carciofo* by Francesco Susini (1641), named after a bronze artichoke centrepiece now lost. At the top of the entrance ramp is the large semi-elliptical **amphitheatre** built by Giulio and Alfonso Parigi in 1630-5 over a garden laid out by Ammannati, in 1599, in imitation of a Roman circus. The elaborate performances held by the Medici in the amphitheatre were meant to glorify the family in no uncertain terms, and often involved exotic animals and dramatic effects of sound and lighting.

A series of terraces rises above the amphitheatre. Turning east (left) as you ascend from the Pitti you come shortly to the Rococo **Kaffeehaus** (open all year except mid-winter) (1), built by Zanobi del Rosso for Pietro Leopoldo in 1775 and frescoed by Giuseppe

Boboli Gardens

del Moro, Giuliano Traballesi and Pasquale Micheli. The *Fontana di Ganimede* (2) on the lawn below is a copy of the 16c original attributed to Stoldo Lorenzi.

The *Neptune Fountain* (3) was created as a fish pond by Stoldo Lorenzi in 1571. Above it rises a colossal statue of *Plenty* begun by Giambologna and finished by Pietro Tacca. The terraces continue to ascend to the **Museo delle Porcellane** located in the 17c Casino del Cavaliere. The rooms contain 18c-19c Italian, French and German

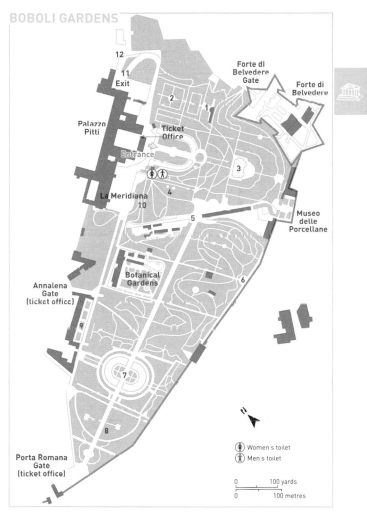

BOBOLI GARDENS

12

11
Exit

2

1

Forte di
Belvedere
Gate

Forte di
Belvedere

Palazzo
Pitti

Ticket
Office

Entrance

3

La Meridiana
10

4

5

Museo
delle
Porcellane

Annalena
Gate
(ticket office)

Botanical
Gardens

6

9

7

8

Porta Romana
Gate
(ticket office)

N

Women's toilet
Men's toilet

0   100 yards
0   100 metres

porcelain from the Medici and Lorraine collections.

Turning west (right), as you ascend from the palace, at the Neptune Fountain you reach the **Prato dell'Uccelare** (4), a lawn shaded by cedars of Lebanon and commanding magnificent views. From here the long, wide, **Viottolone** (5), laid out by Giulio Parigi after 1609, descends steeply through the lower gardens, shaded by tall cypresses. Statues of the *Four Seasons* stand like sentinels at the first crossing; to the left is a colossal bust of *Jupiter* (6) by Giambologna; to the right, are the **botanical gardens** (open in summer).

The impressive **Vasca dell'Isola** (7), a ring-shaped pool originally intended for the cultivation of citrus fruits and flowers, surrounds the **Isolotto**, a small island dominated by the immense *Fontana dell' Oceano*. Tribolo designed the fountain for Cosimo II de' Medici, and Giambologna carved the Neptune figure (copy; the original is in the Bargello). The capricorns guarding the gates are emblems of Cosimo II.

The pathway continues westward to the **hemicycle** (8), a large green shaded by tall plane trees and adorned with two Roman columns carrying Neoclassical vases.

Return to Palazzo Pitti along the north (left) side of the garden, passing the greenhouse and the **orangery** (9), built by Zanobi del Rosso in 1777-8. The green-and-white colour scheme is original. Beyond the Via Romana gate you come to the **Palazzina della Meridiana** (left) and a green hillside with a Roman statue of *Pegasus* (right; 10). On the other side of the palace the path descends gently toward the exit, passing Valerio Cioli's 16c *Fontana del Bacco* (11) where the role of wine god is played by the dwarf of Cosimo, Pietro Barbino; and the **Grotta Grande** (12; shown on request), created after 1574 for Francesco I by Bernardo Buontalenti. The niches at the sides of the entrance to the grotto hold statues of *Apollo* and *Ceres* by Baccio Bandinelli (1552-6); Michelangelo's *Slaves* stood in the corners until 1924, when they were replaced by copies.

on route

Cappella Brancacci, Santa Maria del Carmine, Piazza del Carmine, *T* 055 238 2195. Open Mon, Wed–Sat 10.00–17.00; Sun 13.00–17.00; closed Tues, Easter, 1/5 and 25/12. €3.10.

A few blocks south of Palazzo Pitti lies the modest Carmelite church of Santa Maria del Carmine, whose Brancacci Chapel displays some of the more powerful early 15c frescoes in Florence. The frescoes (c 1425–7) were begun by **Masolino**, who was joined a little later by his protégé **Masaccio**.The decoration of the chapel was interrupted when they departed for Rome in 1428 and was completed in 1485 by Filippino Lippi.

The question of which frescoes were painted by Masaccio and which by Masolino has been a matter of dispute. It is now generally thought that Masaccio was responsible for the *Expulsion of Adam and Eve* (or Expulsion from Paradise), *Baptism of the Neophytes, The Tribute Money, St Peter Enthroned, St Peter Healing the Sick with His Shadow, St Peter Distributing Alms*, and part of the *Resurrection of the Son of Theophilus*.

Museo della Specola, Via Romana 17. Open daily except Wed 9.00–13.00. €5, *T* 055 228 8251. In 1775 Grand Duke Pietro Leopoldo established an astronomical observatory (La Specola) in this building, which is now home to a museum of natural history, famous for its collection of over 600 anatomical wax models. An artist, Clemente Susini, and a physiologist, Felice Fontana, collaborated from 1775 to 1814 to make these 3D visualizations, surely among the more extraordinary objects in Florence. On the ground floor is the Sala degli Scheletri, with carefully restored 18c displays of animal skeletons.

Piazzale Michelangelo is part of a Romantic promenade, known as Viale dei Colli, laid out amidst the low hills south of the city by Giuseppe Poggi in 1860. The outlook over the city and its valley to the Apennine Mountains beyond embraces some of the more celebrated (and photographed) sights in the world. The monument to Michelangelo (1875) in the centre of the piazzale is dominated by one of the city's two reproductions of artist's *David* (the original is in the Accademia).

Santa Felicita, Piazza Santa Felicita. There has been a church on this site for nearly 2000 years. The first was a hiding place and burial ground for the city's first Christians. In 1736 it was thoroughly remodelled by Ferdinando Ruggieri. Inside, in the first chapel on the right, are three magnificent works by **Pontormo**: the intensely emotional *Deposition* over the altar, the *Annunciation* on the right wall, and the *Evangelists* in the pendentives of the cupola (the *St Mark* is attributed to Bronzino). The charming choir (1610-20) is by Cigoli.

San Miniato al Monte

San Miniato al Monte Strikingly situated on a hilltop overlooking Florence, San Miniato is the finest Romanesque church in Tuscany. Its construction began in 1013; the gorgeous marble façade was added towards the end of that century. With its choir raised on a platform above the large crypt, the interior is like no other in the city, and its general form has changed little since the mid-11c.

The church is known for its fine 13c mosaic of *Christ between the Virgin and St Minias*; for the intricately patterned panels of its pavement (1207); for the tabernacle, designed by Michelozzo (1448); and for the memorial chapel of the Cardinal of Portugal, James of Lusitania (who died in Florence in 1459), a collaborative effort of Brunelleschi's pupil **Antonio Manetti** (the architect), **Antonio Rossellino** (who carved the tomb), and **Luca della Robbia** (polychrome ceramic decorations).

According to a medieval legend, St Minias, persecuted by the Emperor Decius and decapitated in the amphitheatre, carried his head across the river and up the hill to this place - a sort of Sleepy Hollow *ante literam*.

Santo Spirito Piazza Santo Spirito is the heart of the Oltrarno, and it is the square connoisseurs of Florence often say they love most. The church of Santo Spirito was built in 1436-87 on the site of an earlier Augustinian monastery to a design by **Brunelleschi**. The modest voluted façade was applied in the 17c. The slender bell tower is 16c.

Brunelleschi's calm, rational interior with its soaring forest of columns is home to some important paintings, notably **Filippino Lippi**'s *Madonna* and Child with the Young St John and Saints ('*Nerli Altarpiece*'), possibly his finest work. **Andrea Sansovino** designed the architecture and carved the sculptures in the Corbinelli Chapel (1492). A door under the organ, in the north aisle, leads through a vaulted vestibule (1492-6), built by Cronaca to a design by **Giuliano da Sangallo**, into the octagonal sacristy (1489-92), also designed by Sangallo, where you can see a painted wood *Crucifix* attributed to **Michelangelo**. (9.00-14.00, closed Mon.)

commercial galleries

Centro Culturale il Bisonte, Via del Giardino Serristori 13r, *T* 055 234 6768, www.ilbisonte.it. Born in 1960 as a printmaking workshop for blue-chip artists, Il Bisonte is now a famous printmaking school. The gallery has prints by Italian and international Modern masters such as Calder, Carrà, Folon, Moore, Picasso, Severini, Sofici and Sutherland.

La Corte Arte Contemporanea, Via Coverelli 27r, *T* 055 284 435. New work by young Italian and international contemporary artists.

Sergio Tossi Arte e Comunicazione, Via Pindemonte 63, *T* 055 228 6163. Opened in 2001 in an old industrial space just outside the Porta Romana, this cutting-edge gallery specializes in artists of the latest generation, principally painters and photographers: Matteo Basile, Alessandro Barzan, Andrea Di Marco, Giacomo Costa, Arnold Dall'O, Fulvio Di Piazza, Max Rohr and others.

Tornabuoni Arte, Lungarno Cellini 13, *T* 055 681 2697. Classic Modernism from Cubism onward: Futurism, Surrealism, Pop Art, Minimalism; works by international artists of the calibre of Chagall, Miró and Picasso; Italians such as Balla, Boccioni, Severini, Soffici, Fontana, Manzoni and Burri.

eating and drinking

The Arno's left bank still has the feel of a village - it almost seems a different city, smaller and more intimate than the Florence of the great monuments, sophisticated shops and bustling crowds. A bohemian place, the Oltrarno holds some of the city's better restaurants. Piazza Santo Spirito is a nerve centre of summer nightlife.

AT THE GALLERIES

Boboli Gardens, *T* 055 218 741. The Rococo **Kaffeehaus**, built by Zanobi del Rosso for Pietro Leopoldo in 1775 and frescoed by Giuseppe del Moro, Giuliano Traballesi and Pasquale Micheli, is a working café, open as the garden (except in the dead of winter) for hot and cold drinks, snacks and light lunches.

Palazzo Pitti, *T* 055 239 8006. Managed by legendary caterer Doney, the museum café at Palazzo Pitti is in Ammannati's great courtyard, a setting of incomparable drama and magnificence. You can sip coffee or drinks, or eat snacks, sandwiches and salads beneath the colonnade, or in a pleasantly furnished room inside.

RESTAURANTS

€ **Al Tranvai**, Piazza Torquato Tasso 14r, *T* 055 225 197; closed Saturday, Sunday and in August. One of the few authentic *trattorie* remaining in San Frediano, frequented by Florentines for its excellent traditional cuisine and lively atmosphere.

Ashoka, Via Pisana 86r, *T* 055 224 446; closed midday. Indian food.

Borgo Antico, Piazza Santo Spirito 6r, *T* 055 210 437; always open. Pizza and simple Tuscan food in rustic atmosphere with summer seating on the square.

Cavolo Nero, Via d'Ardiglione 22, *T* 055 294 774; closed Sunday. Delicious, affordable vegetarian fare.

I Raddi, Via Ardiglione 47r, *T* 055 211 072; closed Sunday. Old-fashioned Florentine *trattoria* in the heart of Oltrarno; the steaks are especially good.

Osteria Santo Spirito, Piazza Santo Spirito 16r, *T* 055 238 2383; always open. Small, fashionable restaurant offering creative interpretations of Tuscan and Italian cuisine; summer seating on Florence's most picturesque piazza.

Ruggero, Via Senese 89r, *T* 055 220 542; closed Tuesday, Wednesday and late July-early August. Just a couple of blocks from Porta Romana, neighbourhood *trattoria* serving great potato *gnocchi*, *ribolita* (in winter), *pappa al pomodoro* (summer), and a variety of (mainly red) meats. No credit cards.

€€ **Alla Vecchia Bettola**, Viale Ludovico Ariosto 32r, *T* 055 224 158; closed Sunday, Monday, in August and late December-early January. Typical Tuscan *osteria*.

Angiolino, Via Santo Spirito 36r, *T* 055 239 8976; closed Wednesday. A fine old Tuscan *trattoria* with great food and open views into the kitchen.

Cammillo, Borgo Sant'Jacopo 57r, *T* 055 221 427; closed Wednesday and Thursday, August and late December-early January. Classic *trattoria*.

Celestino, Piazza Santa Felicita 4r, *T* 055 239 6574; closed Sunday (November-March). Tuscan cuisine, with an emphasis on mushrooms and truffles; also good vegetarian dishes.

Del Carmine, Piazza del Carmine 18r, *T* 055 218 601. Closed Sunday and two weeks in August. Humble neighbourhood *trattoria* with first-rate food and tables on the piazza in summer.

La Loggia, Piazzale Michelangelo 1, *T* 055 234 2832; closed Wednesday and in August. Unexpectedly good food, given the location overlooking Piazzale Michelangelo. You pay for the views.

Mamma Gina, Borgo Sant'Jacopo 37r, *T* 055 239 6009; closed Sunday and two weeks in August.

Momoyama, Borgo San Frediano 10r, *T* 055 291 840; closed Monday and two weeks in August. Fine Japanese cuisine and inventive specialities, elegant atmosphere and valet parking.

Osteria del Cinghiale Bianco, Borgo San Jacopo 43r, *T* 055 2154 706; closed Wednesday. Traditional Tuscan country cuisine, including boar, mushrooms, truffles, roast meats.

Osteria dell'Olio, Piazza dell'Olio 10r, *T* 055 211 466; closed Wednesday. Typical Tuscan fare.

€€€ **Omero Via Pian dei Giullari**, 11r, *T* 055 220 053; closed Tuesday and in August. In the hills above San Miniato al Monte, this traditional Florentine *trattoria* is well worth the walk up from the city; you enter through a small grocery store; the panorama out the back window wall or from the garden terrace (in summer) is as sumptuous as the food.

WINE BARS

€ **Antica Mescita San Niccolò**, Via San Niccolò 60r, *T* 055 234 2836; closed Sunday and in August. Cold meats, cheeses, simple meals and an excellent selection of wines served in an 11c crypt in winter, at outside tables in summer.

Le Volpi e l'Uva, Piazza dei Rossi 1r, *T* 055 239 8132; closed Sunday, holidays and one week in August. Italian and French cheeses, truffles, and hard-to-find wines from small vintners, all in a quiet little square not far from the hustle and bustle of the Ponte Vecchio.

Pitti Gola e Cantina, Piazza Pitti 16, *T* 055 212 704; closed Monday. All the finest Italian wines plus delicious savoury snacks and light meals, with smashing views of the Palazzo Pitti and its square.

€€ **Enoteca Pane e Vino**, Via San Niccolò 70a/r, *T* 055 247 6956; closed midday, Sunday and two weeks in August. Another pleasant place with good food and wine, in the trendy San Niccolò area.

Fuoriporta, Via Monte alle Croce 10r, *T* 055 234 2483; closed Sunday and in August. Best in summer, when you can enjoy great hot and cold meals and delicious wines at the sidewalk tables just outside the magnificent Porta San Niccolò.

CAFÉS

€ **Cabiria**, Piazza Santo Spirito 4r. A night spot popular with the under-30 crowd.

Café la Torre, Lungarno Benvenuto Cellini 65r. Bar with jazz concert series.

Caffè Notte, Via delle Caldaie 28r. Where you go when you can't sleep ...

Dolce Vita, Piazza del Carmine 6r. A good place to meet friends before a night on the town; now also serving meals.

Hemingway, Piazza Piattelina 9r. Specializing in chocolate: pralines, mousses and creams by Italy's finest chocolate makers.

Il Rifrullo, Via San Niccolò 53-57. Good at all hours, including breakfast.

Mr. Jimmy's, Via San Niccolò 47. Everything you miss from America: cookies, brownies, New York cheesecake and much, much more.

Ricchi, Piazza Santo Spirito 9r. Fashionable café with summer seating on the square.

Sottosopra, Via dei Serragli 48r. Another fashionable meeting place for young Florentines.

Zoé, Via dei Renai 13r. Nice cocktails and light lunches, served in a shady square in fair weather.

shopping

Its long history as an artisan's quarter still sets the dominant tone of the Oltrarno today. Wandering the streets you can peek into the shops of carpenters and wrought-iron workers, shoemakers and antiques dealers. The city's better antiques dealers line the Via Maggio (others are in the Via dei Fossi, near Santa Maria Novella). There is a reason for this, too: when the Medici resided at Palazzo Pitti, their peers built elegant townhouses on this street. It is still one of the more impressive in town.

ACCESSORIES

Madova, Via Guicciardini 1. The hand-finished gloves in this family-run shop, each lined in a choice of silk, wool or cashmere, have been famous since 1919.

ANTIQUES

Albrici e Paderni, Via Serragli 20-22r. Furniture, paintings, objets d'art, sculpture.

Arredamento Antico, Via Maggio 16. Furniture, paintings, objets d'art, sculpture.

Galleria Prever, Via Maggio 77r. Art and antiques.

Gallori Turchi, Via Maggio 12-14r. Furniture, majolica, porcelain, paintings, arms and armour.

Giorgi, Via dei Serragli 115r. One of Florence's more venerable antiques dealers (established 1853).

Manlio Agliozzo, Via Maggio 24r. Furniture, paintings, objets d'art, sculptures.

Patrizio Giaconi, Via Maggio 43r. Furniture, paintings, sculpture, objets d'art.

Simone Berti, Via Romana 76r. Antiques, especially French.

Tettamanti, Via Maggio 22r. Furniture, paintings, objets d'art.

BOOKS

City Lights, Via San Niccolò 23. Lawrence Ferlinghetti's San Francisco bookshop transplanted to Florence: English and American literature and criticism.

CRAFTS

Arti & Mestieri d'Oltrarno, Piazza Santo Spirito. Crafts fair, 2nd Sun of the month.

THE HOME

Antico Setificio Fiorentino, Via Bartolini 4. Fine silk fabrics.

Lisa Conti, Via de' Bardi 58. Fabrics for home furnishings as well as original ready-to-wear clothes and accessories.

SHOES

Roberto Ugolini, Via Michelozzi 17. In a shop that looks like it's from another age, with generations of Florentine shoemakers going about their craft in strategically placed black-and-white photographs, this savvy young artisan makes custom footwear to traditional high standard.

Santa Maria Novella

OPEN	**Church**, Mon-Thur & Sat 9.30-17.00; Fri & Sun 13.00-17.00
	Museo & Chiostri Monumentali, Mon-Thur & Sat 9.00-17.00; Sun 9.00-14.00
CLOSED	Museo & Chiostri Monumentali, Fri
CHARGES	**Church**, €2.60; **Museo & Chiostri Monumentali**, €2.60
TELEPHONE	055 282 187
WWW.	smn.it
	comune.firenze.it/servizi_pubblici/arte/musei/b.htm
MAIN ENTRANCE	Piazza Santa Maria Novella
DISABLED ACCESS	Yes
GUIDED VISITS	Audio tours available
SERVICES	Bookshop

The earliest documentary evidence of a chapel that stood on the site of present-day Santa Maria Novella dates from 983: a little country oratory called Sancta Maria in Vineis (Our Lady of the Vineyards) had been built during the Longobard period outside the northwest Roman wall. By 1090 the building had become unsafe and had to be rebuilt; in October 1094 a new and bigger church, called Santa Maria Novella ('New St Mary's') to celebrate the renovation, was consecrated.

In 1221, the year of St Dominic's death, the cathedral chapter gave this Romanesque church to a group of Dominicans who had come to Florence two years earlier. Headed by Blessed Giovanni da Salerno, this small community created such a following that the new premises soon became inadequate. When, in 1244, Pietro da Verona, one of the more renowned preachers of the time, came to Florence, the uninterrupted flow of faithful wishing to attend his sermons obliged the city authorities to create a large space in front of the church façade and spurred the monks to think about the advantages of a new sacred edifice.

The church we see today was begun in 1246; in 1279 construction started on the nave and aisles. The great square in front of the church was opened up in 1288, and at the same time a new and larger circuit of defensive walls was erected to protect the suburbs outside the city gates as well as various religious communities, including Santa Maria Novella.

HIGHLIGHTS

Italian Gothic architecture; Renaissance marble façade by Alberti	Buildings
Sculpture by Bernardo Rossellino, Giambologna, Giuliano da Sangallo, Filippo Brunelleschi and Bernardo Buontalenti Paintings by Cimabue, Filippino Lippi, Domenico Ghirlandaio, Agnolo Bronzino, Nardo di Cione and Masaccio	Interior
Paintings by Paolo Uccello and Andrea di Bonaiuto	Cloisters

THE CHURCH

The design of the church is attributed to two Dominican lay brothers, Fra' Sisto Fiorentino and Fra' Ristoro da Campi, who directed the first phase of construction. Over the next 70 years they were followed by five other master builders, most notably by Fra' Jacopo Talenti da Nipozzano, who also built the Spanish Chapel. By 1360 the essential parts of the church had been completed.

EXTERIOR

The broad, bright façade was begun in 1300. The lower part was probably designed by Jacopo Talenti, in a style mid-way between the Romanesque (visible in the rounded arches of the blind arcades) and the Gothic (evident in the ogival arches above the side doors and the *avelli*, or aristocratic tombs, set into the wall). The marble facing stopped half-way up and the rest of the façade remained bare - like the façades of Santa Croce, Santa Maria del Fiore and other Florentine churches. The decision to complete the work probably dates to the time when Pope Eugene IV resided at

Santa Maria Novella

Santa Maria Novella (mid 15c) and **Leon Battista Alberti** was among his retinue.

The commission to complete the upper part of the façade (1456-70) and the central doorway was given to the young Alberti by one of the more influential Florentines of the time, banker Giovanni di Paolo Rucellai. Alberti applied his Renaissance and Humanistic vision to the pre-existing Gothic elements with magnificent intuition, achieving a perfect harmony of structure and composition.

Two green-and-white striped pilasters contain the lower part of the façade, with the aid of slender Corinthian columns that appear again at the sides of the doorway. A rounded arch encloses the elegant door, adorned by a relief of leaves and flowers that develops on three successive levels. Above the pilasters you can see the ring with the ostrich feather that is the emblem of Nannina Rucellai, daughter of Piero de' Medici; and on the cornice above the columns you can see the logo of the Rucellai bank - a sail set to the wind.

The whole composition is crowned by the tympanum with the sun, the flaming monogram of Christ, at its centre. In the frieze below the tympanum's entablature you can just make out the name, Giovanni di Paolo Rucellai, and the date 1470. The magnificently tarsiated volutes at the sides are an ingenious innovation of Alberti's to cover the aisle roofs and connect the lower part of the façade with the upper part.

INTERIOR

The present appearance of the church interior is the product of a renovation carried out by **Giorgio Vasari** in 1565-7 and of a 19c 'restoration'. The vast, harmonious space combines the vertical thrust of Gothic architecture with an astonishing breadth of proportion. The Latin-cross plan takes up the Cistercian scheme imported to Italy in the 13c and presents a nave and two aisles divided by compound piers that carry pointed arches and cross vaults. The interval between the piers diminishes towards the altar, creating a sense of greater depth and perspective foreshortening when viewed from the entrance. To the right of the doorway is an *Annunciation* (1) of the 14c Florentine school; to the left, another *Annunciation* (2) by Santi di Tito (1538-1603).

SOUTH SIDE The walls of the side aisles are lined with 19c Gothic Revival altars surmounted by slender lancet windows. In the second bay of the south aisle, next to the altar, is the marble *Tomb of Blessed Villana delle Botti* (3), carved 90 years after her death in 1361 by Bernardo Rossellino. The deceased lies beneath a baldachin held open by two angels; the same motif is taken up again in the *Tomb of Blessed Giovanni da Salerno* (4), founder of the monastery, on the wall to the left of the altar.

A *pietra serena* doorway in the sixth bay leads into the Renaissance **Cappella della Pura** (A) (1474). In the corner, left of the altar, a frescoed lunette shows the *Madonna and Child with St Catherine* from which the chapel receives its name (the fresco was removed from a tomb on the outside of the church). The wooden *Crucifix* is by Baccio da Montelupo.

The south arm of the transept holds, on the right, a small wooden tabernacle (5) with a terracotta bust of *St Anthony* (15c) and three important tombs. high up on the same wall are the *Tomb of Tedice Aliotti* (1336), bishop of Florence; on the left, that of *Aldobrando Cavalcanti*, bishop of Orvieto; and below, the *Tomb of Joseph, Patriarch of Constantinople*.

Steps at the end of the transept ascend to the **Rucellai Chapel** (B). On the landing, the *Tomb of Paolo Rucellai* (15c) is a simple sarcophagus. On the altar, where Duccio di Buoninsegna's splended *Rucellai Madonna* was located before it was taken to the Uffizi for safekeeping, there is now a marble statue of the *Virgin and Child* by Nino Pisano. On the walls are remains of frescoes by the St Cecily Master. At the centre of the floor is the *Tombstone of Fra' Lionardo Dati*, in bronze, by Lorenzo Ghiberti (1425).

A gilded wrought-iron gate of the 18c takes you into the **Bardi Chapel** (C), originally used by the Confraternita dei Laudesi founded by St Peter Martyr in 1285. The chapel and its elegant mullioned window both belonged to the old church of Sancta Maria in Vineis. The walls are decorated with partially ruined frescoes from the 13c and 14c. The lunettes (with an *Enthroned Virgin*) have been attributed to **Cimabue**.

The **Chapel of Filippo Strozzi** (D) was acquired in 1486 by this eminent Florentine banker. The walls are decorated with frescoes by **Filippino Lippi**, probably begun in 1497 and completed in 1502. The scenes, showing *St John Reviving Drusiana* and *St Philip the Apostle Expelling the Demon*, are rich in theatrical suggestions, a trait unusual in their time. The figures are arranged as though on a stage, along a horizontal line between two pilasters at the sides that look just like wings. Behind the main action extends a sort of painted backdrop on which architectural follies of Classical inspiration stand out against an idealized sky. In the lunettes are *Martyrs and Saints*, in the ceiling vault *Adam, Noah, Abraham* and *Jacob*. Filippino also designed the windows with the *Madonna and Child* and *Sts John and Philip*, as well as the trompe-l'oeil chiaroscuros on this wall. Behind the altar is the *Tomb of Filippo Strozzi*, a sarcophagus with the Virgin, the Child and four angels magnificently sculpted by **Benedetto da Maiano** (1491-3).

CROSSING AND SANCTUARY The magnificent frescoes in the sanctuary or Great Chapel (E) are **Domenico Ghirlandaio**'s masterpiece (1485-90); they were commissioned by Giovanni Tornabuoni, director of the Medici bank in Rome, in memory of his wife.

Orcagna's original mid-14c frescoes had deteriorated considerably when Giovanni Tornabuoni bought the patronage of the chapel in 1485 and hired Ghirlandaio, then at the peak of his career after working in Rome on the decoration of the Sistine

SANTA MARIA NOVELLA

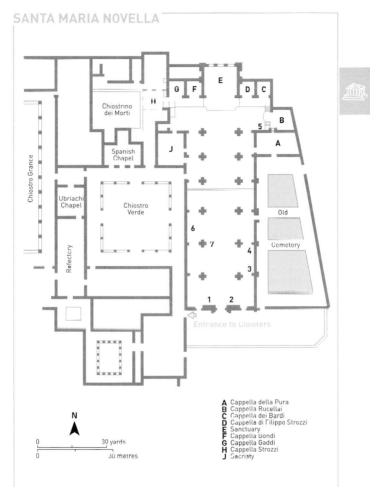

A Cappella della Pura
B Cappella Rucellai
C Cappella dei Bardi
D Cappella di Filippo Strozzi
E Sanctuary
F Cappella Gondi
G Cappella Gaddi
H Cappella Strozzi
J Sacristy

N

0   30 yards
0   30 metres

Chapel, to make a new decorative cycle. With the help of numerous assistants - perhaps including the young Michelangelo - he painted episodes drawn from the lives of the Virgin and of St John the Baptist, very probably following Andrea Orcagna's original design.

These amazing stories provide a fascinating portrait of contemporary Florentine society. Celebrities of the artist's time appear as witnesses to the religious scenes, which take place in 15c Florentine settings. The cycle, on which Ghirlandaio worked for four years, soon became the most exemplary work of its time and an essential part of the studies of the artists who would become the great masters of the century to follow.

NORTH SIDE The **Gondi Chapel** (F) was built by **Giuliano da Sangallo** in white and black marble and red porphyry. On the ceiling are 13c frescoes by Greek painters, who may have taught or inspired Cimabue. On the end wall, under an arch, is **Brunelleschi**'s famous wooden *Crucifix* made, according to Vasari, to show Donatello how Christ on the Cross was meant to be represented; Donatello's *Crucifix*, which Brunelleschi called 'a farm boy on the Cross', is in the Bardi Chapel in Santa Croce.

The **Gaddi Chapel** (G) was built in 1570. Over the altar is Agnolo Bronzino's painting of *Jesus Reviving Jairus' Daughter*.

Steps at the end of the transept lead to the **Strozzi Chapel** (H). This is a very well preserved example of a Tuscan chapel of the mid-14c. The fresco decoration, carefully designed by **Nardo di Cione** in 1357 to cover the entire chapel, draws on the poetic vision of Dante, clearly visible in the dreadful representation of hell. The stained-glass window was designed by Nardo di Cione and by his brother **Andrea Orcagna**, who also made the large altarpiece. This extraordinary triptych, one of the few remaining examples of this artist's work (it is signed and dated 1357), shows *Christ Giving the Keys of the Church to St Peter and the Book of Doctrine to St Thomas*.

Continuing to the left you come upon the beautiful door to the **Sacristy** (J), made by Fabrizio Boschi in 1616. The architecture of the vaulted rectangular interior is the creation of Jacopo Talenti (1350). The room, which was originally a chapel, has a large wooden wardrobe for liturgical objects designed by **Bernardo Buontalenti** in 1582. On the entrance wall hangs **Giotto**'s *Crucifix* of 1290-5. This is an early work, painted on wood and displaying a deep understanding of light and shadow and a strong sense of humanity. On the right of the entrance, in a splendid architectural frame of coloured terracotta, is a marble lavabo by **Giovanni della Robbia** (1497).

Masaccio's Trinity

Masaccio's famous fresco of the *Trinity* (6) occupies the wall at the centre of the third bay of the north aisle. A painted skeleton with the epitaph, 'I was what you are and what I am you will be', has been brought to light below it.

   The painting represents the central mystery of Christian doctrine. The vision of the Trinity - here shown as a Crucifixion rendered in bold perspective, in which Christ is flanked by Mary and John and God the Father looms over the Cross with outstretched arms - is set in an idealized Classical interior. The figures of the patrons, equal in stature to the sacred figures for the first time, propose a human scale both for the architecture and for the concept of God. The horizon line is marked, with obvious symbolic intent, at the level of the step on which the two praying figures kneel. This coincides with the viewer's eye level, so that the skeleton - below, on the transitory level of life and death - appears in profile and foreshortened, whereas the eye must be raised slightly to see the eternal, metaphysical image of divinity. The lines of the composition ascend symmetrically, establishing a triangular hierarchy in which man is the base element and God the apex.

   Unlike Masaccio's earlier frescoes in the Brancacci Chapel in Santa Maria del Carmine, where the naturalistic effects are obtained through a careful manipulation of light and shadow in an essentially painterly composition, here Masaccio opts for frontal lighting and asserts the full importance of powerful drawing aided by scientific exactitude. In fact his adherence to Brunelleschi's rules of perspective (probably formulated in 1425) is so complete as to suggest that the architect had a hand in composing the design.

In a wooden tabernacle in the same bay is a little panel by Davide Ghirlandaio representing *St Lucy*.

The gold-and-marble **pulpit** (7) from which the Dominican fathers denounced Galileo's astronomical theories stands against the next to last pier. It was designed by Brunelleschi and executed by Buggiano in 1443-8.

CLOISTERS AND MUSEUM

A gate on the north side of the façade gives access to the cloisters, now home to one of Florence's more beautiful museums. The first cloister, with tall cypresses around a central well and good views of the campanile, was built around 1350 in the Romanesque style with cross vaults and green-and-white arches on slender columns. It receives its name, **Chiostro Verde**, from the green tone of its decoration. Beneath the arches are numerous frescoes painted with 'green earth' pigment and illustrating the Book of Genesis. Those on the south and west walls are attributed to the early 15c Florentine school.

The frescoes of the east wall were painted by **Paolo Uccello** and his assistants. Removed for restoration following the severe damage caused by the flood of 1966, the frescoes were returned to their place in 1983. The discovery of new techniques permitted the restorers to recapture the reddish tints and halftones that Paolo Uccello used to create the chromatic counterpoint that distinguishes his frescoes from the others. Art historians believe that Paolo Uccello executed the frescoes of the first and fourth bays personally and generally agree that he designed the others. Because of the considerable stylistic difference between the Creation scenes of the first bay, and those of Noah in the fourth, many scholars believe that the artist painted the first before his journey to Venice in 1425, and the second after his return in 1430 - perhaps as late as 1460. The scenes of Noah are generally considered among the artist's greater paintings. In the *Flood*, which is undoubtedly his masterpiece and one of the more disturbing paintings of the Florentine Renaissance, Uccello turns the rules of perspective on their head to give a subjective and psychological reading of reality in severe contrast with the prevailing conception of linear order and logic, introduced by Brunelleschi and ideally expressed in Masaccio's fresco of the *Trinity*.

SPANISH CHAPEL The north side of the cloister gives access to the former **chapter house**, built between 1345 and 1355 by Jacopo Talenti, with funds provided by the merchant Buonamico de' Guidalotti, and frescoed in 1365 by **Andrea di Bonaiuto** (called Andrea da Firenze) and his assistants. In 1566 it was given to Grand Duchess Eleonore of Toledo (wife of Cosimo I de' Medici) as a place of worship for the Spanish members of her retinue.

Andrea's frescoes are the most important work of this otherwise little-known artist; the pictorial decoration is perfectly integrated with its architectural setting. The ceiling vault holds the *Resurrection, Ascension, Navicella* and *Descent of the Holy Ghost*; the altar wall, the *Via Dolorosa, Crucifixion* and *Descent into Limbo*. The *Mission, Works and Triumph of the Dominican Order* appear on the right wall, where you can see the Church Militant with the pope, the Holy Roman Emperor and Church dignitaries standing before the artist's rendering of Florence Cathedral (which was under construction at the time the scenes were painted). Cimabue, Giotto, Boccaccio, Petrarch and Dante stand to the right of the dais behind the kneeling figures in the foreground. At the lower right St Dominic, with St Peter Martyr (the name by which Pietro da Verona has been known since his murder in 1252) and St Thomas Aquinas, dispatches the 'Hounds of the Lord' (a pun on the Order's name, *Domini canes*) to sniff out unorthodox beliefs. Above them lighthearted dancers encircle four seated *Vices* while a Dominican confessor shows the way to the Gates of Paradise, beyond which Christ sits in judgement surrounded by the Heavenly Host.

The opposite wall shows the *Triumph of Church Doctrine* represented by St Thomas Aquinas enthroned beneath winged *Virtues* and flanked by *Doctors of the Church*. The *Life of St Peter Martyr* on the entrance wall has been badly damaged; the apse contains later (and less distinguished) works by Alessandro Allori and Poccetti. Over the altar is a *Madonna and Saints* by Bernardo Daddi; the lovely choir stalls are adorned with female allegories and historical figures representing the Arts and Sciences.

UBRIACHI CHAPEL Built by Francesco Talenti in 1365, this chapel displays detached frescoes of *Prophets* by Andrea Orcagna, from the vault of the family chapel in the church, and the *sinopie* of early frescoes by Paolo Uccello from the east walk of the Chiostro Verde.

REFECTORY This large room on the west side of the cloister was also designed by Talenti. Beneath its beautiful cross vaults are fragmentary frescoes and cases displaying vestments and liturgical objects belonging to the monastery.

on route

Ognissanti, Piazza Ognissanti. Begun in 1261, the church of Ognissanti (All Saints) has been rebuilt several times over the centuries and contains some interesting artworks; but the real draw is in the monastery, entered by a door (no. 42) on the left of the façade. Here, in the pretty vaulted Refectory, with its *pietra serena* lavabos and pulpit, are three Renaissance masterpieces: **Domenico Ghirlandaio**'s *Last Supper* (1480), his *St Jerome* (1481) and **Botticelli**'s *St Augustine's Vision of St Jerome* (1481).

Palazzo Rucellai

Palazzo Rucellai, Via della Vigna. The great architect Leon Battista Alberti broadly defined beauty as 'the harmony and concord of all the parts, achieved in such a manner that nothing could be added, taken away or altered'.

The basic elements of his design for the Palazzo Rucellai (1452?–70?) are the same as those used by Michelozzo in the Palazzo Medici (p 121). But in Alberti's design these features have been absorbed into an over-all system of proportions. The three storeys are of equal height. The rustication, made of smooth blocks of stone, is identical in all three storeys. Most important of all, it is not allowed to assert itself as the dominant element of the structure, but is held in check by a superimposed architectural screen of pilasters supporting entablatures. This Classical screen architecture, having no structural function, established for the Renaissance observer the erudition of the Humanist patron and the Humanist architect. It was the first time Classical orders had been applied to a palace façade.

Piazza Santa Maria Novella. Large obelisks, resting on bronze tortoises, mark the limits of the chariot race established here by Cosimo I in 1563; at the far end of the square is the graceful, post-Brunelleschian **Loggia di San Paolo** (1489-96), with a terracotta lunette over the doorway by **Andrea della Robbia**.

Ponte Santa Trìnita may well be the most elegant bridge in Europe. It was built in 1567 for Cosimo I by **Ammannati** who may have asked Michelangelo's advice on the design: the curve of the volutes is borrowed from his Medici tombs in San Lorenzo (p 117). The bridge was destroyed by bombing in 1944 and rebuilt after the war exactly as it had been before. Much of the original stone was retrieved from the Arno.

Santa Trìnita, in the piazza of the same name, is one of the older churches in Florence. First mentioned in a document of 1077, it was rebuilt in the late 12c, becoming one of the earlier examples of Gothic architecture in Florence.

   Domenico Ghirlandaio painted the magnificent cycle of frescoes telling the *Story of St Francis* in the Sassetti Chapel (1483-6; at the end of the north aisle), and Bernardo Buontalenti added the Mannerist façade in 1593-4.

commercial galleries

Biagiotti Arte, Via delle Belle Donne 39r, *T* 055 214 757. Italian and international contemporary art, especially of the latest generations.

eating and drinking

Many of Florence's more interesting restaurants lie outside the high-rent district between the Duomo and the Arno. The neighbourhood of Santa Maria Novella, especially between the church and the river, offers a good selection of places to eat.

RESTAURANTS

€ **Coco Lezzone**, Via del Parioncino 26r, *T* 055 287 178; closed Sunday and late July-early August. Known among Florentines for its excellent interpretations of traditional Tuscan dishes. Good value for money. No credit cards.

Sostanza, Via del Porcellana 25r, *T* 055 212 691; closed Saturday, Sunday and in August. Traditional Tuscan *trattoria*. No credit cards.

€€ **Buca Lapi**, Via del Trebbio 1r, *T* 055 213 768; closed Sunday, midday Monday and in August. In the cellars of Palazzo Antinori, traditional cuisine and atmosphere.

Buca Mario, Piazza Ottaviani 16r, *T* 055 214 179; closed Wednesday and in August. Typical florentine *buca*, in the cellars of Palazzo Niccolini, a favourite with Florentines for over a hundred years. Tuscan cuisine.

Cantinetta Antinori, Piazza Antinori 3, *T* 055 292 234; closed Saturday, Sunday, in August and late December-early January. In the cellars of historic Palazzo Antinori, elegant and somewhat pricey restaurant serving Tuscan delicacies.

Fonticine, Via Nazionale 79r, *T* 055 282 106; closed Sunday, Monday and late December-early January. Traditional Tuscan dishes; known for its fresh pasta.

I Quattro Amici, Via degli Orti Oricellari 29, *T* 055 215 413; always open. Fish restaurant.

I Tredici Gobbi, Via del Porcellana 9r, *T* 055 239 8769; closed Sunday, Monday and in August. Classic Tuscan cuisine, Liberty (Art Nouveau) interiors.

Il Latini, Via del Palchetti 6r, *T* 055 210 916; closed Monday, early August, and late December-early January. Traditional *trattoria* in the former coach house of Palazzo Rucellai and famous for its *bistecca alla fiorentina*; often crowded, with queues out the door.

Il Profeta, Borgo Ognissanti 93r, *T* 055 212 265; closed Sunday and two weeks in August.

La Carabaccia, Via Palazzuolo 190r, *T* 055 214 782; closed Sunday and midday Monday.

€€€ **Don Chisciotte**, Via Cosimo Ridolfi 4-6r, *T* 055 475 430; closed Sunday and Monday. Great food (especially fish and grilled meats), excellent wines, impeccable service and good ambience.

Osteria No. 1, Via del Moro 18/20, *T* 055 284 897; closed Sunday, midday Monday and in August. Elegant restaurant in a historical old building; famous for its perfect Tuscan cuisine.

CAFÉS

€ **Art Café**, Via del Podestà 29r. Popular with university students.

Capocaccia, Lungarno Corsini 12r. *A la mode* early-evening meeting place.

Rose's, Via del Parione 26. Stylish sushi bar.

shopping

Via del Tornabuoni is Florence's most elegant shopping street. Here, and in the roughly perpendicular Via della Vigna Nuova, you'll find the shops of famous Italian designers, as well as some newcomers you may not have heard of. No visit to Florence is complete without a stop at the Antica Farmacia di Santa Maria Novella (once the monk's pharmacy and now a key place for soaps, perfumes and the like) if only to admire the exquisite décor.

ACCESSORIES

Bottega Veneta, Via dei Tornabuoni 7. An astonishing collection of fashionable handbags plus ready-to-wear leather jackets, tailored skirts, trousers and sweaters, all in the historic Palazzo Gianfigliazzi.

Desmo, Piazza Rucellai 10. Eclectic handbags, exotic shoes and an eccentric line of accessories.

Furla, Via della Vigna Nuova 28. One of the more venerable Italian leather-goods and accessories labels, now also making handcrafted women's footwear.

Giotti, Piazza Ognissanti 3-4. High-end canvas and leather travel cases and bags, as well as excellent quality leather jackets, trousers and skirts made to order in just a few days by real Florentine artisans.

Hermès, Piazza Antinori 6. Every product displayed in this former pharmacy - scarves, porcelain, jewellery, shoes and ready-to-wear fashions for men, women and pets - bears the mark of the French house of Thierry Hermès.

ANTIQUES

Antichità Gonnelli, Via del Moro 32-36r. Furniture, paintings, objets d'art, sculptures.

Casa Blanca, Via dei Fossi 41r. 20c furniture and objets' d'art.

Parronchi, Via dei Fossi 18r. 19c and 20c paintings and furniture.

Velona Antichità, Via dei Fossi 31r. Antique furniture and paintings.

BOOKS

Assolibri, Via del Sole 3r. Books on contemporary art, graphic design and photography, in Italian, English, German, French and Spanish.

BM Bookshop, Borgo Ognissanti 4r. Books in English.

Librairie Français de Florence, Piazza Ognissanti 1. French-language bookstore.

CLOTHES

Agnona, Via dei Tornabuoni 3. Super-soft cashmere, silk, angora and alpaca made by Ermenegildo Zegna, one of Italy's finer makers of fabrics and clothing.

Allegri, Via dei Tornabuoni 27. The Italian rain specialist: waterproof coats and jackets featuring innovative materials and cutting-edge designs.

BP Studio, Via della Vigna Nuova 15. The best wool, cashmere and cotton goes into the creations of these architects-turned-fashion designers, who spice their designs with ethnic influences.

Dolce & Gabbana, Via della Vigna Nuova 27. Contemporary Baroque is the best description for the designs of these two Sicilians, whose large store is as exuberant as the clothes it sells.

Emilio Pucci, Via dei Tornabuoni 20-22. Innovative variations on the vibrant, colourful prints that made this Italian women's label famous.

Enrico Coveri, Via dei Tornabuoni 81. Colour, colour, colour distinguishes Coveri's main line of women's apparel as well as the You Young diffusion line of jeans, T-shirts, sweaters and jackets.

Ermenegildo Zegna, Piazza Rucellai 4-7. Italy's finest and most comfortable menswear and accessories, tucked away in a quiet corner away from the hustle and bustle.

Etro, Via della Vigna Nuova 50. Luxury ready-to-wear fashions and accessories for men and women, elegantly quartered in the former stables of the Rucellai palace.

Gai Mattiolo, Piazza Santa Trinita 1. Not just extravagant styles, but also some extremely wearable pieces from the eccentric Roman designer of women's apparel.

Giorgio Armani, Via dei Tornabuoni 48. Worth exploring just for its maze-like sandstone-lined interior, this is the flagship store of Mr Less-is-More in Florence; exceptional men's and women's fashions, plus cosmetics and perfume, eyewear and watches.

Gucci, Via dei Tornabuoni 73. Men's and women's ready-to-wear lines – and not just in leather.

Il Giglio, Via Borgo Ognissanti 64. Somewhat out of the way, but offering good discounts on designer labels (Dolce & Gabbana, Moschino, Prada, Versace and others) that make the walk worthwhile.

Lacoste, Via della Vigna Nuova 33. The famous polo tops in a seemingly endless variety of shades and a complementary range of men's and women's sportswear and underthings.

Liverano & Liverano, Via dei Fossi 37-42. Men's tailors famous for their shirts and suits made from fine fabrics, especially Italian and English wools and tweeds.

Loro Piana, Via della Vigna Nuova 37. The ultimate in cashmere softness; ready-to-wear for men and women as well as homewear and sumptuous accessories.

Massimo Rebecchi, Via della Vigna Nuova 26. A Tuscan designer creating men's and womenswear with a sleek new urban look, accompanied by a wide range of accessories and shoes.

Mercato delle Cascine, Viale Lincoln, Parco delle Cascine. Open-air market of clothes and housewares, much loved by the Florentines; weekly, Tues morning.

Mila Shon, Via della Vigna Nuova 32-34. This Milanese designer is known for her beautifully crafted sculptural knits and woollens - all for women in this store, with just a few accessories *pour homme*.

Prada (men), Via dei Tornabuoni 67. That unmistakable Prada flair characterizes every one of the suits, shirts and shoes in this store - not to mention the travel bags, wallets, and other stylish accessories.

Prada (women), Via dei Tornabuoni 53. Just a few steps away from the Prada mensware store on the bustling Via dei Tornabuoni are Prada's women's favourites, with their plush fabrics and unusual cuts.

Reporter, Via dei Tornabuoni 47-49. One of the better menswear shops in Italy, rightly famous for its lightweight wool suits, pure cotton shirts, fine-gauge knits and good range of accessories.

Roberto Cavalli, Via dei Tornabuoni 83. To say Roberto Cavalli's ready-to-wear designs for men and women are wild and wacky is a gross understatement; but then in Italian one is crazy not 'as a loon', but 'as a horse' (*cavallo*).

Trussardi, Via dei Tornabuoni 34-36. New children's and babywear collections and a very cool line of scooter accessories now flank Trussardi's traditional, colourful women's and men's ready-to-wear.

Valentino, Via della Vigna Nuova 47. The best of women's ready-to-wear and couture from the Valentino collections, plus the Garavani accessories collection.

Versace, Via dei Tornabuoni 13. Versace's ready-to-wear collections for men (basement) and women (ground floor), including a section of evening dresses that can be made to order.

Yves Saint Laurent, Via dei Tornabuoni 29. The Yves Saint Laurent and Rive Gauche lines of men's and women's ready-to-wear garments; also leather goods and handmade bags.

FOOD

Procacci, Via Tornabuoni 64. Rare delicacies of all kinds to take home, and delicious truffle sandwiches served over the counter.

THE HOME

Arte della Seta, Via dei Fossi 45. Fine silk and other fabrics.

Casa Blanca, Via dei Fossi 41r. Furniture and objects.

Richard Ginori, Via dei Rondinelli 17. A full selection of houseware from the famous Florentine ceramics house.

KIDS

Anichini, Via del Parione 59. Where Florentines traditionally go for high-end children's chothes.

Baroni, Via dei Tornabuoni 9. Everything your kids might need, from clothes (le Petit Bateau skirts and tops, Oshkosh denims, and Baroni's own line of dresses made from Liberty fabrics) to linens and blankets - all made from hand-finished natural fabrics.

Prenatal, Piazza della Stazione 59r. Everything for mums and kids.

LINGERIE

Calzedonia, Piazza della Stazione 1. Sexy and affordable lingerie, hosiery and underthings

La Perla, Via della Vigna Nuova 17-19. Lingerie so decadent it's a shame to cover it up; delicate fabrics and intricate lace in designs ranging from the sweet and demure to the bold and racy

Loretta Caponi, Piazza Antinori 4r. If you've always wondered where Madonna buys her lingerie, well, now you know; but there are any number of graceful, refined things here, too

Wolford, Via della Vigna Nuova 93-95. The upmarket Austrian lingerie and hosiery maker now also makes bodies, nightwear, slips and vests.

PERFUME

Antica Farmacia di Santa Maria Novella, Via della Scala 16. Possibly the most beautiful and refined shop in Florence, making men's and women's soaps, scents, creams, lotions and natural remedies in keeping with a tradition that goes back to the 14c.

SHOES

Bonora, Via del Parione 11-15. Famous for men's and women's custom-made shoes, which may take several months to make and deliver; for those in a rush there is a ready-to-wear line too.

Casadei, Via dei Tornabuoni 33. With some of the more flamboyant designs anywhere, this is the place to shop for the shoes of the stars.

Cesare Paciotti, Via della Vigna Nuova 14. Shoes don't get any more extravagant than these: among the more tame designs, black sneakers embroidered with Swarovski crystals and golden-studded cowboy boots.

Hogan, Via dei Tornabuoni 97. Florence's English Pharmacy used to occupy these premises, now home to the quiet elegance of Diego Della Valle's Hogan footwear and accessories for men, women and children.

Salvatore Ferragamo, Via dei Tornabuoni 14 (women), Piazza Santa Trìnita (men). Worth a visit even if you're not looking for shoes or accessories, the Ferragamo store occupies the historic Palazzo Spini (beautiful frescoed ceilings) and is hung with black-and-white photographs of the Hollywood stars wearing you know what; upstairs is a museum of Ferragamo creations that rivals the Museo del Costume in Palazzo Pitti (visits by appointment).

SPORT

Athletes World, Via dei Cerretani 26-28. A wide range of sportswear and accessories for men and women, plus edgy streetwear - denim jeans and skirts, cargo pants, sweatshirts and tops, and footwear.

Il Rifugio Sport, Piazza Ottaviani 3 and Via dei Fossi 67. Two floors of the biggest names in sportswear for men, women and children, plus a wide range of equipment.

STATIONERY

Il Papiro, Lungarno Corsini 16r and Piazza dei Rucellai 8r. Florence's leading handmade paper shop, selling beautiful stationery, giftwrap, bound notebooks, cards, and more.

Pineider, Via dei Tournabuoni 76r. Florence's finest stationery and writing accessories.

SAN MARCO

Museo di San Marco

OPEN	Tues-Fri 8.15-13.50; Sat 8.15-18.50; 2nd and 4th Sun 8.15-19.00; 1st, 3rd and 5th Mon 8.15-13.50
CLOSED	1st, 3rd and 5th Sun; 2nd and 4th Mon; 1/1, 1/5, 25/12
CHARGES	Full price €4; booking (optional) €1.55 There is a 50% reduction for 18-25-year-olds from the EU and for accredited teachers. Admission is free for young people under 18, school groups (participants must be listed on school letterhead), accredited journalists, those accompanying the disabled, and EU citizens over 60
TELEPHONE	**055 238 8608**
WWW.	**firenzemusei.it**
MAIN ENTRANCE	Piazza San Marco 3
DISABLED ACCESS	Yes (ask at Reception)
GUIDED VISITS	Can be organized by contacting the Education Department of the Curator's Office (**T 055 238 8658**), or the booking service (**T 055 294 883**). Audio tours available
SERVICES	Bookshop

The convent and cloisters of San Marco were Cosimo il Vecchio's greatest gift to Florence. Cosimo bought the grounds for the Dominican monks of Fiesole in 1436 and chose Michelozzo and Fra' Angelico to build and decorate the new convent. The site had been occupied by a medieval monastery of the Silvestrine Order, which had fallen into ruin. Michelozzo used as much as possible of the old buildings to create a monastery whose rooms and layout would be in line with Renaissance criteria of functionality, sobriety and elegance. His only work of genius was transmuted by Angelico into a supremely noble expression of balanced Christianity: sincere, compassionate, mystic, learned. Today the quiet, superbly maintained monastery is one of the more charming museums in Florence.

   San Marco witnessed one of the turning points in Florence's history. By the end of the 15c Florentines had been swung off centre into a hectic, puritanical religiosity incited by Savonarola, who became Prior of San Marco in 1491. The Medici were expelled in 1494, and Jesus Christ was proclaimed King of Florence, with Savonarola acting as political leader. In 1498 the crowds who had wallowed in the demagogue's charisma turned against him. San Marco was besieged, and Savonarola was captured, tried and burned at the stake in the Piazza della Signoria.

In 1869 the suppressed convent of San Marco became a museum honouring the delightful 15c 'primitive' painter, Fra' Angelico. Today it is a nearly complete compendium of his oeuvre. Most of his greatest panel paintings have been assembled here, brought from churches, guilds, and other galleries including the Uffizi, which now retains only two Angelicos. During the 1980s new sections of the convent were opened as a museum housing fragments salvaged from the old parts of the city demolished in the 1860s.

HIGHLIGHTS

Architecture by Michelozzo	Buildings
Panel paintings by Fra' Angelico	Hospice
Frescoes by Fra' Angelico	Dormitories

GROUND FLOOR: THE COMMUNAL ROOMS

The ground floor is taken up by the rooms formerly used for community life: the pilgrims' hospice by the entrance, the chapter house, the refectory and the adjoining kitchen facilities, all arranged around two fine cloisters.

CLOISTER OF SANT' ANTONINO From the vestibule you enter the cloister, a continuous portico with five lowered arches per side, on Ionic columns supported by a low wall. At the centre of the enclosed garden an ancient cedar of Lebanon provides a perfect vertical accent as well as a forceful symbolic presence: according to a symbolism derived from the apocryphal *Book of Wisdom*, Christ is the fruit of the Tree of Life, and Mary is a cedar of Lebanon, a cypress on Zion, a palm in Cades and a rose tree in Jericho.

MUSEO DI SAN MARCO
Ground Floor

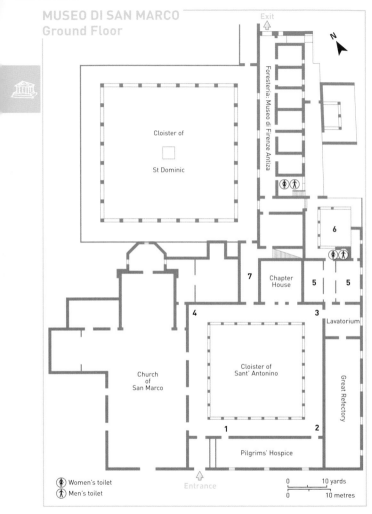

Exit

N

Cloister of

St Dominic

Foresteria: Museo di Firenze Antiza

6

7   Chapter
     House   5   5

4   3

Lavatorium

Cloister of
Sant' Antonino

Great Refectory

Church
of
San Marco

1   2

Pilgrims' Hospice

Entrance

Women's toilet
Men's toilet

0   10 yards
0   10 metres

The cloister takes its name from the monastery's founder, Prior Antonino Pierozzi, who became Archbishop of Florence in 1466 and was canonized in 1523. His life is illustrated in 28 lunettes, by Bernardino Poccetti and other fashionable painters of the 17c, on the cloister's exterior walls. In the corners are frescoes by Angelico: *St Thomas Aquinas* (1), *Christ as a Pilgrim Welcomed by two Dominicans* (2); *Pietà* (3); the mystically beautiful *St Dominic at the Foot of the Cross* and a lunette of *St Peter Martyr* (4).

PILGRIMS' HOSPICE To the right of the entrance is the pilgrims' hospice. This large, vaulted room facing onto Piazza San Marco displays a remarkable collection of masterpieces by Angelico, gathered here from religious buildings in and around Florence. Some are large altarpieces; others are small works whose delicate execution and brilliant colouring recall the miniatures made for illuminated manuscripts. The cult of Angelico as a naive painter stops here – if his spirit was still medieval, his technique was fully informed by the Early Renaissance.

The *Deposition* (1425-32) was commissioned from Lorenzo Monaco by the eminent banker, Palla Strozzi, for the church of Santa Trinita. The artist died in 1425 however, after painting only the cusps and the predella, and Fra' Angelico was asked to finish the work. His rendering of space, and his attention to nature, landscape, physiognomy and emotion combine to make the *Deposition* one of the first masterpieces of the Renaissance. The figure with the black headpiece may be Michelozzo; Palla Strozzi is the gentleman holding the nails and crown of thorns.

The 35 small panels with scenes from the *Life of Christ* (1448-55) originally formed the door of a cabinet for ceremonial silver at Santissima Annunziata. Fra' Angelico conceived the cycle of scenes and painted at least the first nine, using assistants for the others. Many of the compositions appear on a larger scale in the cell frescoes.

On the end wall is the large *Tabernacle of the Linaiuoli*, showing the Enthroned Madonna and Child (1433). Commissioned by the linen-drapers' guild for their headquarters in 1433, the image of the Virgin and Child recalls the Gothic Maestàs of the previous

Fra' Angelico *The Deposition* (detail; 1425-32)

century, but the modelling is stronger and the perspective, clearer. St Mark and St Peter appear on the outside of the door panels, St John the Baptist and St Mark, on the inside. In the predella, scenes of *St Peter Preaching in the Presence of St Mark*, *Adoration of the Magi* and *Martyrdom of St Mark* are described with the liveliness of mystery plays. The marble frame was designed by Lorenzo Ghiberti and executed by two of his assistants.

Of the other paintings, the one made between 1438 and 1445 for the high altar of San Marco - the *San Marco Altarpiece* - is clearly the most magnificent. It was intended to point to Medici patronage of San Marco through the presence of the family's patron saints Cosmas and Damian. The painting was badly damaged by an 18c cleaning, which corroded most of the colour; it nevertheless preserves a remarkable sense of theatricality and scale.

The circular group of conversing saints - the ancestor of the *sacra conversazione* theme so dear to Renaissance patrons and painters - is adapted to the painting's square format by ingenious devices such as the little shrine in the foreground and the geometric design of the rug. These devices correspond exactly to the doctrines of architect Leon Battista Alberti, who had arrived in Florence a few years before and had circulated, only two or three years before this picture was painted, the Italian version of his *Treatise on Painting*.

The perspective construction over rising levels, the lofty central arch, and the pyramidal grouping of figures within a circle seen in depth are the nucleus of Raphael's **School of Athens** in the Vatican; very possibly Fra' Angelico's painting and other centralized, multifigure compositions within an architectural perspective, such as Ghiberti's almost contemporary **Meeting of Solomon and the Queen of Sheba** in the Gates of Paradise (p 7) had a strong influence on the young Raphael when he worked in Florence in the early 16c.

CHAPTER HOUSE Across the cloister is the chapter house, whose external appearance (exposed stone walls and large windows), marks it as part of the 14c monastery. Inside is Angelico's grand, mystic vision of the **Crucifixion** (1442). In this monumental painting the founders of the major religious orders and the Fathers of the Church, as well as saints linked to the Medici, the monastery and the city, are united in a collective meditation on the sacrifice of Christ.

Also in the room are a large sculpted and painted wood **Crucifix** by Baccio di Montelupo (1496) and the monastery bell, commissioned by Cosimo il Vecchio (possibly from Donatello and Michelozzo) around 1445 and later used to rally popular sentiment against the Medici and in defence of Savonarola.

KITCHEN AND REFECTORIES Leaving the chapter house you turn left to enter the *lavatorium*, or wash room, with a ruined fresco of the **Last Judgement** by Fra' Bartolomeo and Mariotto Albertinelli (1499-1501) and works by **Luca** and **Andrea della Robbia**.

From here you reach the **Great Refectory**, originally of the 14c but enlarged in the 15c (by Michelozzo) and 16c. It is hung with works by Fra' Bartolomeo and the 'San Marco School' of painters who followed his example. More works by Fra' Bartolomeo occupy the former **kitchen** (5) located by the little Chiostro della Spesa (6), where suppliers brought their goods to the monastery. A corridor divides this part of the kitchen from another dominated by a large standard from the mid-15c formerly attributed to Baldovinetti, around which are collected 15c paintings by artists influenced by Fra' Angelico. The best of these are Francesco Botticini's large canvas of *St Antonino at the Foot of the Cross* (c 1460), bearing obvious similarities to Angelico's fresco of St Dominic, as well as a debt to the nervous line and anatomical richness of Andrea del Castagno; and Benozzo Gozzoli's lovely little predella panel with the *Mystical Marriage of St Catherine, Christ in the Tomb with St John and Mary Magdalene*, and *St Anthony Abbot* and *St Benedict*. Benozzo studied with Angelico for 20 years.

A vestibule (7) connects the Chiostro di Sant'Antonino to the larger and slightly later Chiostro di San Domenico, which is still occupied by the Dominican monks (hence closed to visitors). To the left, at the foot of the stairs up to the dormitory, is the **small refectory** used originally by monastery guests staying in the adjoining *foresteria*. Now home to the museum bookshop, it holds **Domenico Ghirlandaio**'s clear, descriptive *Last Supper*, 1479-80. The room also contains **Della Robbia** terracottas, notably Andrea della Robbia's *Deposition from the Cross*, 1505-10.

FIRST FLOOR: DORMITORIES AND LIBRARY

Stairs lead up to the first floor dormitories. The 43 cells, each with its own vaulted ceiling, are arranged beneath a single huge wooden roof; they were built before 1443, the year in which Pope Eugenio IV consecrated the new monastery. Here is the famous cycle of frescoes painted by **Fra' Angelico** and his assistants from 1439 to 1445. How many of the frescoes are by the hand of the master alone, and how many are by artists employed in his studio is still unknown. What is certain is that this is one of the larger

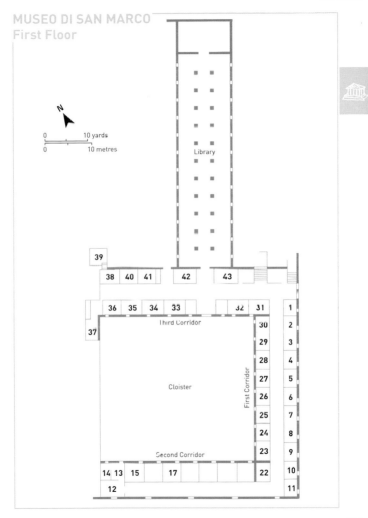

MUSEO DI SAN MARCO
First Floor

N

0   10 yards
0   10 metres

Library

39

38 40 41   42   43

36 35 34 33   32 31   1

37   Third Corridor   30   2

29   3

28   4

Cloister   27   First Corridor   5

26   6

25   7

24   8

Second Corridor   23   9

14 13 15   17   22   10

12   11

Renaissance cycles in existence, combining spirituality and realism, reality and unreality, with a new descriptive language that transformed the cultural heritage of the past without disowning it. The style of these frescoes differs sharply from that of the altarpieces for public view, and there is even a distinction between the frescoes destined for the monastic community as a whole and those in the individual cells. Now, as then, the austere but serene appearance of the dormitory recalls the meditative tone of monastic life, divided into precise prayer and study duties far from the clamour of city life.

At the head of the stairs is Fra' Angelico's *Annunciation* (c 1440), one of the more famous images of Renaissance art and Angelico's best known work. It exemplifies the artist's light, airy painting style, the clarity of Florentine architecture and the descriptive capacity of perspective. The scene is set beneath a simply plastered, bare arcade; the environment recalls the arcade of the cloister just built by Michelozzo on the ground floor of the monastery. There are no decorative elements or subsidiary episodes; the painter clearly wished to concentrate totally on the intimacy and spirituality of the situation.

FIRST CORRIDOR To the left of the *Annunciation* is the Friars' Corridor, built by Michelozzo to house the Dominican brothers who had just settled into the monastery. The first 20 cells, arranged on both sides of the corridor, were completed by 1437 and were frescoed by Angelico shortly afterwards, each with a scene from the life of Christ. The ten paintings on the left were all painted by Angelico, whereas those on the right were designed by the master but often painted by assistants.

SECOND CORRIDOR The seven cells of this corridor that open onto the cloister were reserved for novices. They are all frescoed with images of *St Dominic at the Foot of the Cross*, in attitudes varying from imploration to self-flagellation, thought to have been executed jointly by Angelico and Benozzo Gozzoli. The three rooms at the end of the corridor are thought to be Savonarola's chapel, study and cell.

The cells of the entrance corridor were for special guests. The rooms (38, 39) that were occupied as a retreat by Cosimo il Vecchio, and by Pope Eugene IV when he came to consecrate the monastery in 1443, hold an unfinished *Adoration of the Magi* believed to have been painted by Fra' Angelico with the help of Benozzo Gozzoli.

LIBRARY The library of San Marco was famous for its collection of Greek and Roman authors, many of which were given by Cosimo il Vecchio. The collection was augmented by donations from the Florentine Humanists and catalogued according to a system devised by Tommaso da Sarzana, later Pope Nicholas V. Over the centuries most of the books have been transferred to public libraries, particularly the Biblioteca Laurenziana and the Biblioteca Nazionale. Among the rare manuscripts remaining are a *Missal* probably illuminated by Fra' Angelico while he was still living at San Domenico di Fiesole, and illuminated choirbooks and psalters mostly of the 15c-16c.

The room was designed by **Michelozzo** in the form of a basilica, with three aisles of equal height, the outer ones groin-vaulted, the central one roofed by a barrel vault and supported on an airy arcade of Ionic columns. Despite the constricted space, the slenderness of the elements gives the interior a lightness and delicacy like those of Fra' Angelico's architectural backgrounds. Michelozzo clearly conceived the library as a temple of knowledge, and its aulic atmosphere contrasts sharply with the simplicity of the other rooms.

During restoration work in 2000 the original emerald green colour of the frescoed *intonaco* on the walls and vaults was discovered under four layers of plaster; this can now be seen in several places. At the end of the room is the **Sala Greca**, added in 1457, which preserves a lovely painted ceiling. The cabinets, dating from 1741, now contain vases made in Montelupo in 1570 for the pharmacy of San Marco.

BEFORE LEAVING From the small refectory (see above) at the bottom of the stairs you enter the Museo di Firenze Antica, arranged in the cells of the *foresteria*. Five of the cell doors are decorated by Fra' Bartolomeo with lunettes depicting Dominican saints - St Vincent Ferrer, St Peter Martyr, the Blessed Ambrogio Sansedoni, St Dominic and St Thomas. Here are architectural fragments salvaged from the demolition of the old centre of Florence - arranged in the 19c according to type, in keeping with curatorial criteria of the time. The exit at the end of the vaulted corridor is through a lovely little garden, in an area once part of the convent's extensive vegetable garden.

The adjacent church of **San Marco** (1437-52) was built by Michelozzo, but subsequently altered by Giambologna in 1588 and Pier Francesco Silvani in 1678. The Humanist poet Politian (Angolo Ambrogini, 1454-94) and scholar Pico della Mirandola (1463-94) are buried inside.

Galleria dell'Accademia

OPEN	Tues-Sun 8.15-18.50
CLOSED	Mon; 1/1, 1/5, 25/12
CHARGES	Full price €6.50; booking (optional) €1.55
	There is a 50% reduction for 18-25-year-olds from the EU and for accredited teachers
	Admission is free for young people under 18, school groups (participants must be listed on school letterhead), accredited journalists, those accompanying the disabled and EU citizens over 60
TELEPHONE	**055 238 8609**; booking service **055 294 883**
WWW.	**firenzemusei.it**
MAIN ENTRANCE	Via Ricasoli 60
DISABLED ACCESS	Yes (ask at Reception)
GUIDED VISITS	Can be organized by contacting the Education Department of the Curator's Office (**T 055 238 8658**), or the booking service (**T 055 294 883**). Audio tours available
SERVICES	Cloakroom, bookshop

The collection of the Galleria dell'Accademia consists of works of art from the Accademia del Disegno founded by Cosimo I de' Medici in 1563, and from the Accademia di Belle Arti, an art school founded by Grand Duke Pietro Leopoldo of Lorraine in 1784. The aim of this collection of works was originally to give young artists a place to study and copy the great art of the past. The suppression of religious institutions in 1785 and 1808 brought numerous religious paintings to the gallery, and in 1873 Michelangelo's *David*, previously set on the steps of Palazzo Vecchio, was also moved here. In 1909 it was joined by his *Slaves* and *St Matthew*, and in 1939, by the *Palestrina Pietà*. The gallery has been considerably enlarged since 1980: a collection of plaster casts by the 19c sculptors Lorenzo Bartolini and Luigi Pampaloni has been arranged in the large ground-floor Room of the Tuscans, and a collection of Florentine Gothic paintings has been installed on the first floor, along with a unique group of Russian icons from the private collections of the Grand Dukes of Lorraine.

HIGHLIGHTS

Michelangelo. *Slaves. St Matthew, David*	Ground floor
Paintings by Lorenzo Monaco	First floor
Altar frontal from Santa Maria Novella	

GROUND FLOOR
THE GALLERY OF THE SLAVES AND THE TRIBUNE OF DAVID
This large room is shaped like a Latin-cross church interior, with **Michelangelo**'s *David* at the crossing, in place of the high altar. The wings and the central Gallery of the Slaves occupy pre-existing edifices; the domed Tribune was built expressly for the *David* between 1873 and 1882.

The four *Slaves* or *Prisoners*, sculpted around 1530 for the (unbuilt) tomb of Pope Julius II in St Peter's in Rome, belong to Michelangelo's body of unfinished sculptures. These figures seem to suggest that they are fighting to emerge from the stone. This would imply that their incomplete state was intentional, and there has been a great deal of speculation as to whether the artist drew a deliberate distinction between their aesthetic perfection and their physical completion. He did write a sonnet about how hard it is for the sculptor to bring the perfect figure out of the block in

Michelangelo's David

The 517cm-tall *David* was originally commissioned by the Opera di Santa Maria del Fiore to be placed on the exterior of the cathedral - probably on one of the buttresses of Brunelleschi's cupola. It was sculpted by Michelangelo between 1501 and 1504, during which time the plan to put this and other monumental sculptures on the cathedral was abandoned: after much discussion and debate, the *David* was placed in front of the Palazzo della Signoria, where it became a symbol of the civic freedom and virtue of Republican Florence. It remained in that location until 1873, when it was transferred to the Accademia di Belle Arti.

For this huge statue, an exceptionally large commission in Florence, Michelangelo reused a block of marble left unfinished about 40 years before. The marble was offered to several other artists, including Andrea Sansovino and Leonardo da Vinci, before it was finally assigned to Michelangelo. The modelling is especially close to the formulas of Classical antiquity, with a simplified geometry suitable to the huge scale yet with a mild assertion of life in its asymmetry. This element of Classicism clearly distances Michelangelo's *David* from the statues of the same subject previously made by Donatello and Verrocchio, which, adhering more closely to the biblical text, depicted David as a slender boy unaware of his divine mission. The statue's perfect modelling, the calm and determined strength of the expression, and the imposing size have made it one of the better known and more admired works of art in the world - perhaps the most famous single work of of Western art - and established Michelangelo as the foremost sculptor of his time at the age of 29. It has continued to serve as the prime statement of the Renaissance ideal of perfect humanity.

which it is potentially present. Thus, even if the works remained formally unfinished, their condition reflects the artist's intense feeling of the stresses inherent in the creative process.

THE FLORENTINE ROOMS These three rooms are dedicated to 15c Florentine painting. Among the masterpieces displayed here are **Paolo Uccello**'s *Scenes of Hermit Life* (1460) and **Botticelli**'s *Virgin and Child with the Young Saint John and Two Angels* (c 1468). However, the emphasis is on the everyday production of the more active workshops of Renaissance Florence, for example those of Domenico Ghirlandaio and Cosimo Rosselli. Masaccio's brother, known as Lo Scheggia, painted the busy wedding scene with elegant guests in period dress in front of the baptistery, on the *Cassone Adimari* in the first room.

THE HALL OF THE COLOSSUS The plaster study for Giambologna's *Rape of the Sabine Women* (1582) stands at the centre of this large room, though the name comes from one of Montecavallo's *Dioscuri* displayed here in the 19c.

The paintings are hung in chronological order; they date from the 16c. Among the more notable are the *Descent from the Cross* (1504 and 1507), begun by Filippino Lippi and completed, after the painter's death, by Perugino, who also painted the *Assumption of the Virgin with Saints* (1500); Fra' Bartolomeo's *Prophets Isaiah and Job* (c 1514-5), painted after his return from Rome and making clear reference to Michelangelo's Sistine ceiling; and Andrea del Sarto's detached fresco, *Christ as the Man of Sorrows* (c 1525), from Santissima Annunziata. The room displays some of the musical instruments from the Medici and Lorraine collections, which will be permanently relocated in the museum of the Luigi Cherubini School of Music, next door.

NINETEENTH-CENTURY ROOM This was conceived to provide a stable home for the collection of plaster casts by Lorenzo Bartolini and to offer the visitor tangible evidence of the 19c academic origins of the gallery.

BYZANTINE ROOMS Florentine gold-ground painting is represented in these rooms. The central room has works by 13c and 14c artists; in the left-hand room are the Orcagna family and their close collaborators; in the right-hand room are Giotto's direct followers, Taddeo Gaddi, Bernardo Daddi, Jacopo del Casentino.

FIRST FLOOR

These rooms are dedicated to late Gothic Florentine painting. The first room, which takes its name from Giovanni da Milano, holds the artist's superb *Pietà* of 1365. The collection of 14c paintings in the second room includes portable altarpieces and large polyptychs, as well as the beautifully embroidered *altar frontal* from Santa Maria Novella made by Florentine craftsmen and signed and dated 1336 by Jacopo Cambi.

In the third room is a collection of nine works by Lorenzo Monaco, including the beautiful *Prayer in the Garden*, painted around 1400 for the monastery of Santa Maria degli Angioli where the artist was a monk. The fourth room is devoted to works in the International Gothic Style and the Collection of Russian icons, put together by the Grand Dukes of Lorraine.

San Lorenzo

OPEN	**Cappelle Medicee**, Tues-Sun 8.15-17.00; 1st, 3rd and 5th Sun 8.15-17.00; 2nd, 4th Mon 8.15-17.00
CLOSED	**Cappelle Medicee**, 2nd, 4th Sun; 1st, 3rd and 5th Mon; 1/1, 1/5, 25/12
CHARGES	**Cappelle Medicee**, Full price €6; booking (optional) €1.55 There is a 50% reduction for 18-25-year-olds from the EU and for accredited teachers Admission is free for young people under 18, school groups

(participants must be listed on school letterhead), accredited journalists, those accompanying the disabled and EU citizens over 60

TELEPHONE	**Cappelle Medicee**, T **055 238 8606**; booking service **T 055 294 883**
WWW.	**firenzemusei.it**
MAIN ENTRANCE	**Cappelle Medicee**, Piazza Madonna degli Aldobrandini 6
DISABLED ACCESS	Yes (ask at Reception)
GUIDED VISITS	Can be organized by contacting the Education Department of the Curator's Office (**T 055 238 8658**), or the booking service (**T 055 294 883**). Audio tours available
SERVICES	**Cappelle Medicee**, cloakroom, bookshop

San Lorenzo is more than just a church. It is almost a city within a city, teeming with history, as grand in its structural complexity as it is in its size. Its origins coincide with those of the Christian era. A church dedicated to St Lawrence was consecrated here in 393 by St Ambrose, then bishop of Milan. In 1418 Giovanni di Bicci de' Medici radically enlarged and renovated this primitive building and San Lorenzo remained the favoured parish and church of the Medici for over 300 years. It was here that the lords of Florence and Tuscany, whose first palace was just round the corner, celebrated the weddings and baptisms of their dynasty; here they attended the great ceremonies of state, and here they buried their dead.

HIGHLIGHTS

Architecture by Brunelleschi **Interior decoration by Donatello**	Church
Architecture by Brunelleschi (Old Sacristy) **and Michelangelo (New Sacristy)** **Medici tombs by Michelangelo**	Sacristies
Architecture and furnishings by Michelangelo	Laurentian Library

THE CHURCH

To build their parish church the Medici hired **Brunelleschi** for the first and only time. He conceived the vast, rational and harmonious buliiding you see today, though he did not live to see it completed. The commission to build a façade was given to Michelangelo, and there are drawings, writings and a wooden model conserved in the Museo di Casa Buonarroti (p 148) that give an idea of the grandness of his design. Unfortunately the vicissitudes of history kept the project from ever taking form. In 1520 the contract was rescinded, and only the interior façade was completed.

INTERIOR The vast, luminous interior is one of the more understatedly powerful in Italy, designed by Brunelleschi in 1420 and completed by Manetti in 1460. The delay was caused by financial crises in the Medici banks, but it is evident that money was not stinted on the final construction: even the *pietra serena* trim was carved by leading sculptors of the day. If the San Lorenzo structures are considered keystones of the early Renaissance architectural style, it is not because the church departed from the traditional basilican form with nave, side aisles, and apse. What Brunelleschi added to the conventional format was a new vocabulary using his own interpretation of antique designs for the capitals, friezes, pilasters, and columns. His design as a whole was one of unusual regularity, where the separate parts of the church rationally corresponded to each other and created a profound visual and intellectual harmony.

The original wooden ceiling has been restored; on the west wall is a small balcony, built by Michelangelo (1530) for Clement VII, for the exhibition of the Holy Relics kept in the treasury. In the south aisle are Rosso Fiorentino's *Marriage of the Virgin* (1) of 1523 and Desiderio da Settignano's *Ciborium* (2), carved around 1461, perhaps for the high altar of the church.

Donatello's magnificent bronze **pulpits** (3 and 4) stand atop Ionic marble columns. These, the sculptor's last works, were finished by his pupils Bertoldo and Bartolomeo Bellano (c 1461-5). The

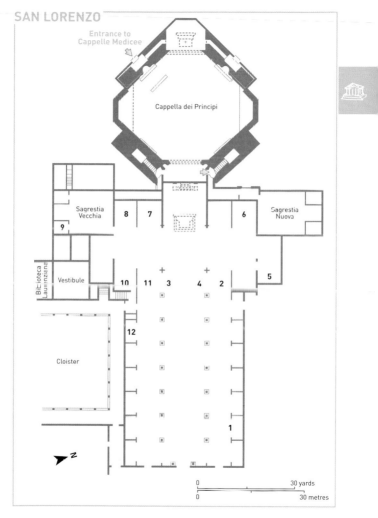

SAN LORENZO

Entrance to
Cappelle Medicee

Cappella dei Principi

Sagrestia
Vecchia

8 7

6

Sagrestia
Nuova

9

Biblioteca
Laurenziana

Vestibule

10 11 3

4 2

5

12

Cloister

1

N

0   30 yards

0   30 metres

Pulpit of the Passion (3), on the north side of the nave, depicts the sacrifice of Christ as narrated in the gospels. The scenes in chronological order recount the *Agony in the Garden, Christ before Pilate* and *Christ before Caiaphas*, the *Crucifixion*, the *Lamentation* and the *Descent from the Cross.* The back was completed in the 17c with wooden reliefs of the *Flagellation* and *St John the Evangelist*. The *Pulpit of the Resurrection* (4), on the south side of the nave, represents the *Entombment*, the *Descent into Limbo*, the *Resurrection*, the *Ascension* and the *Pentecost* - though not in strict chronological order. On the back is a relief showing the *Martyrdom of St Lawrence*, signed by Donatello and dated 1465, and 17c wood reliefs of *St Luke* and the *Mocking of Christ*. In these superlative masterpieces by Italy's greatest sculptor after Michelangelo, the counter-melody of the Florentine Renaissance, anti-Classical and visionary, emerges with particular force.

At the foot of the high altar - created in the 18c, in *pietre dure*, by Gaspare Maria Paoletti and incorporating a panel of the *Fall of Manna* by Bernardino Poccetti - three round grilles in the pavement and a simple inscription with the Medici arms mark the grave, in the crypt, of Cosimo Il Vecchio (d. 1464). Above the altar is a *Crucifix* by Baccio da Montelupo. The dome was frescoed by Vincenzo Meucci (1742).

The transept chapels contain, among other works, a Roman sarcophagus (5) and two 19c funerary monuments by Leopoldo Costoli (6), one to the goldsmith Bernardo Cennini, who printed the first book in Florence in 1471, the other to the painter Pietro Benvenuti; a 14c painted wood statue of the *Madonna and Child* (7); a beautiful painting of *Saints Anthony Abbot, Leonard and Julian* (8) by the school of Domenico Ghirlandaio; and a 19c monument to Donatello (10), who died in 1466 and is buried in the vault below. The sculptor probably carved the marble sarcophagus of Niccolò and Fioretta Martelli (c 1464), opposite; the painting of the *Annunciation* is a beautiful early work of **Filippo Lippi** (1437-41), in which the principles of Renaissance perspective theorized by Leon Battista Alberti and applied ten years earlier by Masaccio in the Brancacci Chapel (p 67 are treated with poetic lyricism.

Bronzino made the large fresco of the *Martyrdom of St Lawrence* in the north aisle (11); the large modern painting of *Christ in the Carpenter's Workshop* (12) is by Pietro Annigoni.

THE SAGRESTIA VECCHIA

Inlaid doors in the north transept lead to the Sagrestia Vecchia (Old Sacristy), built at the expense of Giovanni di Bicci de' Medici. Brunelleschi's early masterpiece (1421-8). This is one of the first mathematically conceived architectural spaces of the Renaissance: a perfect cube completed by a hemispherical umbrella dome.

Donatello's sculptural decorations, carried out in the 1430s, consist of the four polychrome medallions illustrating scenes from the *Life of St John the Evangelist* in the pendentives; the four polychrome tondos of the *Evangelists* in the lunettes; the Medici saints, *Cosmas* and *Damian, Stephen* and *Lawrence*, in the lunettes over the bronze doors flanking the apse; and the doors themselves, with figures of the *Martyrs* (right) and *Apostles* (left) facing each other. Donatello was responsible for the architecture of the doors as well as the bronze relief panels.

Left of the entrance is **Verrocchio**'s exquisite *Monument to Piero and Giovanni de' Medici* (1472), whose volutes are cited by Leonardo in the Uffizi *Annunciation*. In the small dome of the apse is a singular representation of the Florentine sky as it was on 6 July 1439, the date of the successful conclusion of the Council of Florence between the Greek and Roman churches. It has been attributed to Giuliano d'Arrigo (called Pesello). The terracotta bust of *St Lawrence* (or St Leonard) has been attributed to Donatello or Desiderio da Settignano. The wood furnishings are decorated with fine inlay; In the centre is the sarcophagus of Giovanni di Bicci de' Medici (d. 1429) and Piccarda Bueri, the parents of Cosimo il Vecchio, by Buggiano (c 1443). The beautifully carved *lavabo* in the little chapel left of the altar (9) has been attributed to Donatello, Desiderio da Settignano, Antonio Rossellino and Verrocchio.

THE BIBLIOTECA LAURENZIANA

From the north aisle or from a doorway at the left of the façade, on Piazza San Lorenzo, you enter the graceful **cloister**. A staircase on the side by the church ascends to the Biblioteca Laurenziana. This library was designed by **Michelangelo** in 1524-34, to house the collection of Classical and Humanist manuscripts founded by Cosimo il Vecchio, later removed to Rome by Leo X and finally returned to Florence by Clement VII who commissioned the building you see today.

The **vestibule** contains Michelangelo's most famous and original wall designs. The bold and free rearrangement of traditional building components goes beyond structural requirement - for instance, to place columns recessed behind a wall plane rather than in front of it as is usual. This has led to the work's being cited as the first instance of Mannerism as an architectural style, when Mannerism is defined as an approach that intentionally contradicts the classical and the harmonious, favouring expressiveness and originality. The **staircase**, which fills nearly the entire room, was left unfinished by Michelangelo and completed in the 1550s by Vasari and Ammannati.

Biblioteca Laurenziana vestibule

By contrast the long **library** room is far more restrained, with traditional rows of desks neatly related to the rhythm of the windows and the decorative detail in the floor and ceiling (designed by Michelangelo's pupil Tribolo, with the Medici motifs of the ram's skull and the motto '*Semper*'). At the far end of the long room, opposite the stairway, another door led to a space intended to hold the library's rarest treasures. It was to be a triangular room, a climax of the long corridor-like approach. The *Medici Virgil* is among the codices displayed.

THE CAPPELLE MEDICEE

The Cappelle Medicee (Medici Chapels) are approached from outside the east end of the church; the entrance is in Piazza Madonna degli Aldobrandini.

CAPPELLA DEI PRINCIPI The ideas of Death and Power in the time of Catholic absolutism find their most splendid manifestation in the Chapel of the Princes, the mausoleum of the Medici grand dukes. Designed by Cosimo I's illegitimate son Giovanni de' Medici, and by Bernardo Buontalenti, this gloomy, portentous shrine was built by Mateo Nigetti after 1602. Clad entirely in dark marbles and semi-precious stones, it was the most expensive of all Medici building projects and the one that posterity was to judge as being the least successful. The octagonal ground plan is based on that of the baptistery and, like that building, associates the number eight with the concept of eternity.

SAGRESTIA NUOVA The New Sacristy was **Michelangelo**'s first realized architectural creation, begun in 1520 and left unfinished when he left Florence for Rome in 1534.

The chapel was created by Pope Leo X to honour his father, Lorenzo il Magnifico, and his uncle, Giuliano de' Medici, and to strengthen the authority of these dukes' bastard heirs Giuliano, Duke of Nemours, and Lorenzo, Duke of Urbino. Another Medici pope, Clement VII, took up the project in 1520, entrusting the design of the architecture and execution of the tombs to the greatest artist of the day.

The New Sacristy is a relatively small room, yet the impression is one of breadth. The architectural space is very simple: a cube topped by a hemispheric dome. It makes obvious reference to Brunelleschi's Old Sacristy, to which it is symmetrical in the layout of the church, but Michelangelo's creation is more tense and dramatic. Here, as in the Biblioteca Laurenziana, Michelangelo has 'sculpted' his architecture, viewing the space as a rival from which to wrest intensely expressive forms.

Against the white-plastered walls, the architect sets a limpid *pietra serena* framework of fluted pilasters, cornices, mouldings and windows with triangular tympana - elements typical of the structural and ornamental language of the time, but used with an unconventional twist. The force and intensity of these structures contradict the calm harmony of surface and space that distinguishes Brunelleschi's work. Michelangelo transforms Brunelleschi's model into a sensational theatre where the drama of the sculptural groups is exalted and intensified. The play unfolds in the lower part of the sacristy, where the sculptures are located. The room here is covered with marble on three sides - a rhythmic chain of twin pilasters, niches, festoons and cornices with masks - imparting a heroic foundation to the architect's contemplation of death.

The entrance wall holds a sculptural group of the *Virgin and Child with Saints Cosmas and Damian*, an allegory of Paradise. The central group was executed by Michelangelo in 1521; *Saints Cosmas and Damian* were carved respectively by his pupils Angelo da Montosoli and Raffaello da Montelupo. At the Virgin's feet, in a simple marble sarcophagus, lie the mortal remains of Lorenzo il Magnifico (d. 1492) and Giuliano de' Medici (killed in the Pazzi Conspiracy of 1478). The monument with which Michelangelo intended to commemorate them was never carried out.

THE MEDICI TOMBS The leading players in the New Sacristy are two cadets of the Medici house, who bear the same names as their illustrious ancestors. On the left is the *Tomb of Lorenzo, Duke of Urbino*; on the right is the *Tomb of Giuliano, Duke of Nemours*.

The effigies of Lorenzo and Giuliano are traditionally described as active and thoughtful, respectively. Rendered as standard types of young soldiers, they were at once perceived not as portraits but as idealized superior beings, both because of their high rank and because they are souls beyond the grave. Both turn to the same side of the room. It has naturally been thought that they focus on the Madonna, which is at the centre of this side wall. The heads of the two figures, however, are turned in differing degrees, and their common focus is in a corner of the chapel: the entrance door from the church. In a word, they are addressing you and me.

Giuliano is bare-headed, dressed in armour and holding the

staff of command. At his feet, spread on the volutes of the sarcophagus, are two allegorical figures, representing *Day* (right) and *Night* (left). *Dawn* and *Dusk* occupy similar positions on the tomb of Lorenzo. Such personifications had never appeared on tombs before, and they refer, according to Michelangelo, to the inevitable movement of time, which is circular and leads to death.

Night is represented as an athletic young woman sleeping with her head on her right hand, while her muscular body turns slightly to one side. She bears the symbols of night: the crescent-moon diadem on her forehead, the dream-inducing poppies at her feet, and the owl, lord of darkness. *Day* is a male figure. His pose is a near mirror-image of *Night*'s, but his gaze is turned outward in an act of dominion, raising the unfinished head as if to represent the indistinct, blinding splendour of the sun as it traverses the heavens. One is accustomed to imagining the sculpture of Michelangelo in black and white. An attentive study of *Day* and *Night* reveals that the artist imparted colour to his marble by finishing the various surfaces differently. The polished body of *Night* glows with a cold, lunar clarity, while the rough surface of *Day*, over which the light dances in amberish tones, seems almost to exude the warmth of the sun.

The companion piece dedicated to Lorenzo, Duke of Nemours, was carried out during Michelangelo's last years in Florence, between 1531 and 1533. Like the imperious, strong-willed Giuliano, Lorenzo is seated, armed and therefore prepared for action; his countenance, however, shows a reflective and meditative demeanour. The allegories of *Dawn* and *Dusk* at his feet once more symbolize the rhythmic flow of time. Just as the fleeting states of day and night impel one to action, so dawn and dusk, moments of transition between light and darkness, offer opportunities for contemplation. *Dawn* seems to awake slowly from a dream, stretching her limbs and shaking off the drowsiness of the night. *Dusk* is a male nude at rest, the unfinished head slightly inclined as if weighed down by the labours of the dying day.

During restoration work in 1978, a group of **charcoal drawings** was found to have been sketched on the walls of the **sacristy**

basement. These may have been made by Michelangelo, who is thought to have hidden here when an order for his execution was issued after the return of the Medici in 1530 (he supported the Republican government of 1527-30). He came out of hiding later in the year when Clement VII requested his pardon. Visits are arranged for small groups (by appointment at the ticket office, 9.00-12.00).

on route

Chiostro dello Scalzo, Via Cavour 69. Open Mon, Thur, Sat 8.15-13.50, *T* 055 294 883. **Andrea del Sarto**'s most famous mural cycle is the *grisaille* (grey monochrome) series of frescoes on the *Life of St John the Baptist*. Begun about 1511, the work was not completed until 1526, and almost all of it was painted by his own hand, so that it reads like an artistic autobiography covering the greater part of his career.

Museo Archeologico, Via della Colonna 38. Open Mon 14.00-19.00; Tues-Thur 8.30-19.00; Wed, Fri, Sat & Sun 8.30-14.00; in summer also on Sat 21.00-24.00. €4, *T* 055 215 270.

The Archaeological Museum provides one of the few opportunities in Florence to step outside the Renaissance. The Etruscan sculptures are an essential and fascinating grounding for those who intend to visit the nearby Etruscan sites; the Greek and Roman collections enhance understanding of the Renaissance art they helped to inspire.

Museo dell'Opificio delle Pietre Dure, Via degli Alfani 78. Open Mon-Sat 8.15-14.00; Tues 8.15-19.00; €2, *T* 055 21010. This museum, devoted to precious-stone (*pietra dura*) and polychrome marble inlay, *scagliola* (imitation marble), paintings on stone, oil paintings and work tools, was founded in 1588 by Grand Duke Ferdinando I, who established the workshop that produced the decoration of the Cappella dei Principi, San Lorenzo. In 1796, Pietro Leopoldo moved the Opificio to its present location in Via degli Alfani. Of particular interest are the Medici coat of arms with putti; a portrait of Cosimo I in *pietra dura* dating from 1597; and an 18c model of the Cappella dei Principi.

Palazzo Medici Riccardi, Via Cavour 3. An outstanding example of secular architecture, the Palazzo Medici (called the Palazzo Medici-Riccardi after its acquisition by the Riccardi family) was created by Cosimo il Vecchio's court architect **Michelozzo** after 1444. The palace is arranged around a central court - the traditional Florentine palace plan - but its design differs considerably from earlier palaces. Medieval Florentine palaces were built of great rusticated blocks of stone, creating an impression of fortification. In Michelozzo's design little regard is shown for military might. The ground floor has the usual heavy rustication, the second floor has smooth blocks outlined by incised lines, and the third floor has ashlar stonework with no indications of the blocks. In addition, Michelozzo crowned his palace with a massive horizontal cornice in the Classical style.

The palace chapel was frescoed from 1459 to 1460 by **Benozzo Gozzoli** with a cycle of paintings showing the *Procession of the Magi*. These, the artist's most popular and imaginative paintings, show the Medici family riding on horseback through a fairytale Tuscan landscape. The chapel can be visited daily except Wed, 9.00-12.00, €8. Optional booking, *T* 055 276 0340.

Piazza Santissima Annunziata is architecturally the most harmonious open space in Florence. The equestrian statue of *Grand Duke Ferdinando I* in the centre of the square is **Giambologna**'s last work, finished in 1608 by his pupil Tacca. It is the subject of Browning's poem 'The Statue and the Bust'. Tacca also made the two small green fountains (1629),

Sant'Apollonia, Via XXVII Aprile. The refectory of this former convent contains **Andrea del Castagno**'s finest painting, the *Last Supper*. Executed around 1450, it is one of the most beautiful and least known works of this influential painter, known for the emotional power and naturalistic treatment of figures in his work. The *sinopia* is exhibited on the opposite wall.

Santissima Annunziata This church was founded after 1240 by the seven original Florentine members of the Servite order. Michelozzo, who was the brother of the Servite Prior, rebuilt the church between 1444 and 1481. Today it is still the favourite of fashionable Florentines.

The atrium (or **Chiostro dei Voti**) is famous for its Mannerist frescoes: Rosso Fiorentino, *Assumption*; Pontormo, *Visitation*; Franciabigio, *Marriage of the Virgin*; Andrea del Sarto, *Birth of the Virgin* and *Coming of the Magi*; Alesso Baldovinetti, *Nativity*; Cosimo Rosselli, *Vocation and Investiture of San Filippo Benizzi*; and five more *Scenes from the Life of San Filippo* by Andrea del Sarto.

Spedale degli Innocenti This hospital for foundlings was **Brunelleschi**'s first major architectural commission (1420s-30s). The ceramic reliefs of swaddled babies (c 1487) are perhaps the best-known works of **Andrea della Robbia**.

The **Galleria dell'Istituto degli Innocenti**, inside, has two beautiful cloisters - the Chiostro degli Uomini and the Chiostro delle Donne. Highlights of the first-floor Pinacoteca include Domenico Ghirlandaio's beautiful *Adoration of the Magi* and Luca della Robbia's glazed terracotta *Madonna and Child* (1445-50). Open 8.30-14.00; closed Wed; *T* 055 249 1708.

commercial galleries

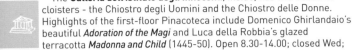

Print Service, Via degli Alfani 15r, *T* 055 234 3640. One of Europe's premier black-and-white photo laboratories, with a small gallery space devoted to cutting-edge contemporary photography.

eating and drinking

Two Florentine institutions characterize epicurian life in the district between the Duomo and San Marco: the Central Market and the University. The area abounds with good, cheap places to eat - some (Il Vegetariano, Caffelatte) to an 'alternative' crowd.

RESTAURANTS

€ **Café Caracol**, Via Ginori 10r, *T* 055 211 427; closed Monday and in August. Good Tex-Mex cuisine, rustic ambience.

Da Nerbone, Mercato Centrale di San Lorenzo, *T* 055 219 949; serving lunch only, closed Sunday and in August. Simple fare in the midst of the hustle and bustle of the central market.

Il Vegetariano, Via delle Ruote 30r, *T* 055 475 030; closed Monday, midday Saturday, Sunday and holidays, in August and late December–early January. Great vegetarian food, including cous-cous, tofu with seasonal vegetables, savoury pies and casseroles, served buffet-style.

Mario, Via della Rosina 2r, *T* 055 218 550; serving lunch only; closed Sunday and in August. Near the Mercato Centrale di San Lorenzo. Informal atmosphere and good simple food are the hallmarks of this well-known *trattoria*. They don't take reservations, so get there early or be prepared to wait. No credit cards.

Palle d'Oro, Via Sant'Antonino 43-45r, *T* 055 288 383; closed Sunday and in August. A meat-eater's restaurant (fillet of beef with porcini mushrooms, steak, *ossobuco*, tripe) by the central market.

Taverna del Bronzino, Via delle Ruote 25/27, *T* 055 495 220; closed Sunday, midday Monday, Christmas, Easter and August.

WINE BARS

€ **Casa del Vino**, Via dell'Ariento 16r, *T* 055 215 609; closed Sunday and in August. Right by the central market, an authentic Florentine wine bar crowded with authentic Florentines; good sandwiches, great wines, fabulous prices.

La Mescita, Via degli Alfani 70r, *T* 055 239 6400; closed Sunday and in August. A hop, skip and a jump from Piazza Santissima Annunziata, this popular place is also close to the University Faculty of Letters. Crowded at lunch time, quiet in the afternoon.

Zanobini, Via Sant'Antonino 47r, *T* 055 239 6850; closed Sunday. If location is everything, then these folks, on the little street that leads from the station to the market, must be billionaires. The food is good enough, and there is a fine selection of wines.

CAFÉS

€ **Brunellesco**, Via degli Alfani 69r. Snacks, sandwiches and light meals in a place bustling with students from the University Faculty of Letters.

Caffèlatte, Via degli Alfani 39r. A good, old-fashioned milk bar, with delicious sweet and savoury baked goods.

Gelateria Carabé, Via Ricasoli 66r. The best Sicilian ice cream, *granita* (fruit slush), and pastries north of Palermo; *cannoli* (pastry shells stuffed with custard or ricotta) are made up *espresso* when you order.

Robiglio, Via dei Servi 112r. Delicious pastries, great coffee and hot chocolate.

shopping

The presence of the city's fabulous open-air market around the church of San Lorenzo influences shops in the neighbourhood, which tend to be bargain-oriented. Also, the proximity of the university allows a number of good bookshops to thrive.

BOOKS

Feltrinelli, Via Cerretani 30r. Italy's leading bookstore chain probably has more books and periodicals in this store than most public libraries: a genuine treasure trove, almost exclusively in Italian.

Feltrinelli International, Via Cavour 12-20r. The multilingual version of Feltrinelli's well-known, well-stocked Italian-language stores, offering double the selection of most American bookshops - including children's books.

Marzocco, Via Martelli 22r. This venerable Florentine establishment takes its name from the city's heraldic lion; the selection is almost as wide as Feltrinelli's.

Mondadori, Via San Gallo 49r. Books in Italian, English, French, German and Spanish.

CLOTHES AND ACCESSORIES

Benetton, Via Borgo San Lorenzo 15. Few know that Benetton collections in Italy differ from those available elsewhere; this megastore has stuff for men, women, teenagers and kids.

Mercato di San Lorenzo. Sprawled out around the basilica of San Lorenzo and in the adjacent Via dell'Ariento, the San Lorenzo market is an obligatory stop for any serious shopper. Its stalls are jam-packed with clothes and accessories of remarkable quality, at surprising prices.

Raspini, Via Martelli 5-7. The best names in Italian ready-to-wear apparel for both men and women.

Sisley, Via dei Cerretani 57. Sporty casualwear as well as more elegant things, for grown-ups and kids, in extremely up-to-date collections by the trendy Parisian fashion label.

Stefanel, Via dei Cerretani 46-48. One-stop shopping for jeans, T-shirts, sweaters and a full range of accessories, well within most budgets.

FOOD

Mercato Centrale, Piazza del Mercato. This is the principal food market in the town and is well worth a visit. The magnificent cast-iron building (1874) was designed by Giuseppe Mengoni, architect of the iron-and-glass *gallerie* in Milan and Naples. Open Mon-Sat 7.00-13.00; also 16.30-19.30 on Sat except in July and August.

THE HOME

Bartolini, Via dei Servi 24. A toy store for grownups who like to play in the kitchen.

Frette, Via Cavour 2. The ultimate place to shop for luxury linens and homewear – and for men and women's pyjamas, robes, and the like.

La Ménagère, Via dei Ginori 8. A fine traditional place to go for kitchenware, ceramics, glass and cutlery.

KIDS

Benetton 0-12, Via dei Cerretani 60-22. Trendy clothing and accessories for the little ones, and a colourful, stylish range of maternity wear.

Dreoni, Giocattoli Via Cavour 31-33r. The largest toy store in town.

MUSIC

Alberti, Via dei Pucci 16r and Borgo San Lorenzo 45r. All sorts of CDs, cassettes and things to play them on.

SHOES

Gilardini, Via dei Cerretani 8 & 20. Hand-finished shoes by Bruno Magli and Santoni, as well as a traditional line bearing the Gilardini label.

Raspini, Via Martelli 5-7. Florence's most famous name in footware.

SPORT

Athletes World, Via dei Cerretani 26-28. A wide range of sportswear and accessories for men and women, plus edgy streetwear - denim jeans and skirts, cargo pants, sweatshirts and tops, and footwear.

Footlocker, Via Borgo San Lorenzo 19. Brand-name trainers plus cool urban and sportswear from Italian houses Fila, Lotto and Umbro.

STATIONERY

Il Papiro, Via Cavour 55r. Florence's leading handmade paper shop, selling beautiful stationery, giftwrap, bound notebooks, cards, and more.

San Lorenzo market

SANTA CROCE

Santa Croce

OPEN	Mon-Sat 9.30-17.30; Sun 13.00-17.30
CLOSED	1/1, 1/5, 25/12
CHARGES	Full price €3 (one ticket gives admission to the Basilica, Cappella Pazzi, Museo and Chiostri) Reduced price €2 (young people 11-18); residents, children under 11 and disabled, free
TELEPHONE	**055 246 6105**
MAIN ENTRANCE	Piazza Santa Croce
DISABLED ACCESS	Yes (ask at Reception)
GUIDED VISITS	Audio tours available
SERVICES	Bookshop

Santa Croce, the church of the Franciscans in Florence, is one of the finest examples anywhere of Italian Gothic architecture. It was begun in 1294, possibly by Arnolfo di Cambio, and was finished in 1442, except for the Gothic Revival façade and campanile, which were added in the 19c. The interior preserves masterpieces of Tuscan Gothic or proto-Renaissance painting by Giotto, Taddeo Gaddi and Agnolo Gaddi. There are examples of sculpture by such masters of early Renaissance art as Rossellino, Donatello, Desiderio da Settignano, Andrea della Robbia, and Benedetto da Maiano. Many famous Italians - Leon Battista Alberti, Michelangelo, Vittorio Alfieri, Leonardo Bruni, Gioacchino Rossini, and Galileo - are buried in the church. One of the finest examples of early Renaissance architecture, the Pazzi Chapel by Brunelleschi, is in the 14c cloister.

The square looks much as it did in the 16c and 17c. The Palazzo dell'Antella (no. 21), designed in 1619 by Giulio Parigi, was frescoed in 20 days by 12 assistants of Giovanni da San Giovanni. Less picturesque but architecturally more forceful is the Serristori-Cocchi Palace (no. 1, opposite the church), attributed to Baccio d'Agnolo. Under Savonarola heretics were burned in this square, and book burnings continued until 1580. Earlier, in the prime years of the Medici, Santa Croce was the setting for elaborate pageants in honour of Lorenzo the Magnificent's betrothal to Clarice Orsini and of Giuliano's love for Simonetta Vespucci.

HIGHLIGHTS

Architecture attributed to Arnolfo di Cambio
Paintings by Giotto, Agnolo and Taddeo Gaddi
Sculpture by Antonio, Bernardo Rossellino,
Donatello, Desiderio da Settignano (nave),
Andrea and Giovanni della Robbia,
Benedetto da Maiano
                                                            Church

Architecture by Brunelleschi
Sculpture by Donatello, Luca della Robbia and
Desiderio da Settignano
                                                            Pazzi Chapel

Cimabue, *Crucifix*, Taddeo Gaddi, *Tree of Life*,
Donatello, *St Louis of Toulouse*
                                                            Museo
                                                            dell'Opera

THE CHURCH

The Franciscan's mission was to teach and preach to the city's poor – of which there were many. The church and its square are therefore quite large, though not ostentatious in the manner of Santa Maria Novella; the overall tone is austere, almost minimalist – in keeping with the Franciscan sense of simplicity.

INTERIOR

The immense interior of Santa Croce is strongly influenced by the Gothic style imported to Italy from France – especially in its older apsidal part, with its polygonal choir and transept chapels covered by tall ogival vaults. But there is an obvious lack of Gothic prettiness: the large wall surfaces are plain and austere; the overall effect, one of spectacular monumentality, in perfect harmony with the Florentine penchant for Classical architecture.

SANTA CROCE

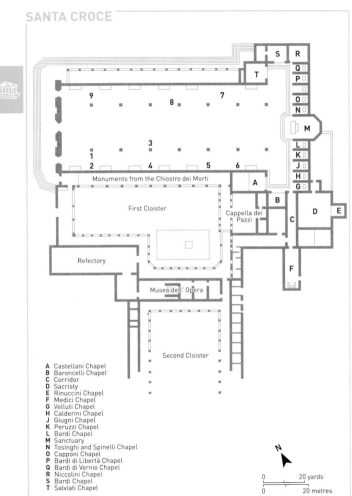

9   8   7

3

1
2   4   5   6

Monuments from the Chiostro dei Morti

A

First Cloister

Cappella dei
Pazzi

Refectory

Museo dell' Opera

Second Cloister

A   Castellani Chapel
B   Baroncelli Chapel
C   Corridor
D   Sacristy
E   Rinuccini Chapel
F   Medici Chapel
G   Velluti Chapel
H   Calderini Chapel
J   Giugni Chapel
K   Peruzzi Chapel
L   Bardi Chapel
M   Sanctuary
N   Tosinghi and Spinelli Chapel
O   Capponi Chapel
P   Bardi di Libertà Chapel
Q   Bardi di Vernio Chapel
R   Niccolini Chapel
S   Bardi Chapel
T   Salviati Chapel

N

0   20 yards

0   20 metres

SOUTH SIDE On the first pier is an exquisite relief of the *Madonna del Latte* by **Antonio Rossellino** (1; 1478). The *Tomb of Michelangelo*, in the bay to the right (2), was designed **Vasari** in 1570 and adorned by minor artists with a bust of Michelangelo, allegorical figures of *Painting, Sculpture* and *Architecture*, and a fresco of the *Pietà*. A beautiful octagonal marble *Pulpit* (3) by **Benedetto da Maiano**, with relief carvings of the life of St Francis and five Virtues (1472-6) flanks the third pier.

The *Monument to Vittorio Alfieri* (4), the poet, is a splendid work by Italy's finest Neoclassical artist, **Antonio Canova** (1810). Further along on the right is the *Cavalcanti Tabernacle* (5), with **Donatello**'s *Annunciation* (c 1435) in gilded *pietra serena*; the architectural surround was designed in collaboration with Michelozzo. The *Tomb of Leonardo Bruni* (6) by **Bernardo Rossellino** is a beautiful and highly influential example of Renaissance sepulchral art inspired by the architecture of Brunelleschi (1444). Bruni was a Humanist scholar and historian, biographer of Dante and Petrarch, a Papal Secretary and Chancellor of the Republic.

The **Castellani Chapel** (A) contains frescoes of scenes from the *Lives of St Anthony Abbot* and *St John the Evangelist* (left) and *St Nicholas of Bari and St John the Baptist* (right) by **Agnolo Gaddi** and assistants (c 1385). The **Baroncelli Chapel** (B) was frescoed in 1332-8 by **Taddeo Gaddi**, Giotto's most faithful pupil. The fresco cycle in the chapel illustrates the *Life of the Virgin*. The altarpiece of the *Crowning of the Virgin* is signed by **Giotto**, but may have been made by members his workshop, including possibly Taddeo Gaddi. Taddeo also painted the four *Prophets* above the entrance arch and the *Madonna and Child* in the lunette of the Gothic tomb of a member of the Baroncelli family (1327) on the lower right.

The adjacent doorway and corridor, designed by **Michelozzo** with inlaid wooden doors attributed to **Giovanni di Michele**, bring you to the beautiful 14c **sacristy** (D), with a 16c intarsiated and inlaid bench chest designed by Giovanni di Michele. The fresco of the *Crucifixion* on the right wall is by Taddeo Gaddi; those of the *Way to Calvary* are attributed to Spinello Aretino, and the *Resurrection* is by Niccolò di Pietro Gerini. Giovanni della Robbia made the bust of the *Redeemer*.

At the far end the **Rinuccini Chapel** (E) is closed by a Gothic wrought-iron gate (1371). It was frescoed around 1365 by **Giovanni da Milano**, a close follower of Giotto from Lombardy, with the *Life of Mary Magdalene* (right) and the *Life of the Virgin* (left). The polyptych over the altar was made by Giovanni del Biondo (1372). The **Medici Chapel** (F) was built in 1434 to a design by Michelozzo. Giovanni di Michele made the fine inlaid door and Andrea della Robbia and his assistants executed the beautiful terracotta altarpiece of the *Madonna and Child with Angels* (c 1480). The frescoes are by Paolo Schiavo (*Madonna with Saints*) and **Spinello Aretino** (*St John the Baptist*). Galileo is buried in this chapel.

EAST END It was probably before going to Naples, around 1329, that **Giotto** painted frescoes in four chapels in Santa Croce belonging to the Giugni (J), Peruzzi (K), Bardi (L) and Tosinghi-Spinelli (N) and families. The Giugni Chapel frescoes are lost, as are all the Tosinghi-Spinelli ones, except for an *Assumption* over the entrance, not universally accepted as by Giotto. The Bardi and Peruzzi chapels contained cycles of *St Francis, St John the Baptist*, and *St John the Evangelist*, but the frescoes were whitewashed and were not recovered until the mid-19c, when they were damaged in the removal of the whitewash and then heavily restored. A prolonged cleaning and re-restoration of both chapels in the mid-20c demonstrated that the **Bardi Chapel** has few but splendid figures remaining, painted in true fresco, whereas the **Peruzzi Chapel** figures are now largely ghosts, as they were painted in a different technique. The older view, that the two cycles were contemporary, is no longer shared by scholars, and there is no evidence for the date of either cycle, except that both are probably later than the Scrovegni Chapel frescoes in Padua (1305). Taddeo Gaddi painted the altarpiece of the *Madonna and Saints* in the Peruzzi Chapel.

The walls and vault of the polygonal **sanctuary** (M) were frescoed with the *Legend of the True Cross* and *Christ*, the *Evangelists* and *St Francis*, around 1380 by **Agnolo Gaddi**. Agnolo also designed the beautiful stained-glass lancet windows. The altarpiece is a 19c reconstruction combining a *Madonna and Saints* by Niccolò Gerini with *Fathers of the Church* by Giovanni del Biondo with a predella including a central panel by Lorenzo Monaco. The *Crucifix* above the altar is a brilliant work of the Master of Figline.

Bernardo Daddi painted the *Lives of St Lawrence* and *St Stephen* in the **Bardi di Libertà Chapel** (P), and **Giovanni della Robbia** made the polychrome terracotta altarpiece. In the **Bardi di Vernio Chapel** (Q) the frescoes illustrating the *Life of St Sylvester* were made by Maso di Banco (1335-8), who also designed the stained glass windows and may have painted the kneeling figure of *Bettino de' Bardi* with Christ receiving his soul into heaven, in the first Gothic tomb. The *Deposition* in the second niche is attributed to **Taddeo Gaddi**. The rich marble decoration of the **Niccolini Chapel** (R) is a remarkable anticipation of the 17c Baroque style, created in 1579-85 by Giovanni Antonio Dosio.

Giotto and Italian Gothic painting

In the 13c Tuscany had a flourishing pictorial tradition strongly influenced by Byzantine art. The transitional period 1250–1300 is poorly documented but, as with all Gothic decorative art, the changes are in the direction of greater realism. By the end of the 13c, painters in Tuscany had discovered the use to which light could be put in figure modelling. The Italian painters also made sudden and unexpected advances in the manipulation of perspective to describe the space of the scenes they were painting. More than this, the best painters developed an extraordinary ability to create figures that really look as if they are communicating with each other by gesture and expression; the work of the Giotto in the Bardi and Peruzzi chapels is an especially good example of this trend.

NORTH SIDE In the **Bardi Chapel** (S) is the wooden *Crucifix* by **Donatello** that Brunelleschi criticized for looking like a 'peasant on the Cross', if Vasari is to be believed (see also p 82). **Desiderio da Settignano**'s beautiful *Tomb of Carlo Marsuppini* (7), of 1453, was inspired by Rossellino's *Tomb of Leonardo Bruni* across the nave; the beautiful Classical sarcophagus may be by Verrocchio.

Marsupini, like Bruni, was a Humanist scholar and Chancellor of the Republic. In the floor by the fourth column (8) is the elegant tomb-slab with the emblem of an eagle that marks the burial place of Lorenzo Ghiberti and his son Vittorio. Galileo's remains were not allowed to be given Christian burial until the 18c: the *Monument to Galileo Galilei* (9) was designed in 1737 by Giulio Foggini and decorated with sculptures by Giovanni Battista Foggini (who carved the bust of the great scientist), Girolamo Ticciati (*Geometry*, right) and Vincenzo Foggini (*Astronomy*, left).

MUSEO DELL'OPERA DI SANTA CROCE

To the right of the church is the entrance to the cloisters, the Pazzi Chapel and the museum. The **first cloister** dates mainly from the 14c. A memorial to Florence Nightingale (who was born at nearby Bellosguardo) is on the right as you go in; on the left are numerous 19c tombstones and on the lawn, amid cypress trees and acanthus plants, a seated figure of *God the Father* by Baccio Bandinelli (now a war memorial) and a statue of a *Warrior* donated by the 20c British sculptor Henry Moore.

THE PAZZI CHAPEL Around 1429 Andrea de' Pazzi commissioned **Brunelleschi** to design a chapel adjacent to Santa Croce that was intended to be a chapter house (a place of assembly for friars to conduct business). Work probably did not begin before 1442 and was not completed until 1460, well after the architect's death.

Brunelleschi used mathematical modules and geometric formulas for the plan and elevation of the Pazzi Chapel, as he had in San Lorenzo, but he arranged the space in a more complex and sophisticated manner in the later building. On the inside it is actually a rectangle, slightly wider than it is deep; at its rear is a square bay for the sanctuary, and at the front is a porch. There are three domes, a large one over the centre of the chapel and small ones over the sanctuary and over the centre of the porch on the exterior. So its plan, but not its interior space, resembles a Greek cross. The creamy wall surface of the Pazzi Chapel is marked off in geometric patterns by dark grey stone.

The clarity, coolness, and elegance for which Brunelleschi's architecture is noted finds a perfect complement in the sober decorative scheme: 12 enamelled terracotta roundels of the seated *Apostles* by **Luca della Robbia** (c 1442-52) adorn the rib-vaulted dome; in the pendentives are four polychrome roundels of the *Evangelists* thought to have been designed by **Donatello** and glazed by the Della Robbia (although some scholars

Santa Croce Pazzi Chapel

attribute them to Brunelleschi). The sanctuary has decorations by the school of Donatello and a stained-glass window attributed to Alesso Baldovinetti.

On the exterior the large dome is covered by a conical roof with a lantern at the top. The porch has a horizontal entablature supported by six Corinthian columns but broken in the centre by a semicircular arch that centralizes the composition, repeats the shape of the dome in the porch behind it, and gives a lift to the horizontal façade. It may have been designed by **Giuliano da Maiano** who, with his brother **Benedetto**, made the great wooden door. In the centre of the barrel vault is a small dome adorned with enamelled terracottas by **Luca della Robbia**, including the Pazzi emblem. Luca also made the medallion with *St Andrew* over the door (c 1461). The frieze of cherubs' heads has been attributed to **Desiderio da Settignano**.

MUSEO DELL'OPERA DI SANTA CROCE The contents of the museum, especially the panel paintings, suffered gravely from the 1966 flood, but the more important works are now on display in the refectory. On the right is **Cimabue**'s large *Crucifix* for the high altar of Santa Croce which was about 70 per cent destroyed in the flood and became the symbol for the disaster and the recovery effort that followed. On the left wall is **Donatello**'s gilt bronze statue of *St Louis of Toulouse,* which was made for Orsanmichele but replaced there by Verrocchio's *Doubting of St Thomas*. Here, too, are detached fragments of a large fresco by **Orcagna** showing the *Triumph of Death* and the *Inferno*, from the nave of the church.

The end wall bears a huge fresco by **Taddeo Gaddi** of the *Tree of Life*, inspired by the writings of St Bonaventura, the biographer of St Francis, and scenes showing the *Last Supper, St Louis of Toulouse, St Francis, St Benedict* and *Mary Magdalene Annointing the Feet of Christ*.

The **second cloister** is entered from the far right-hand corner of the first cloister, past a splendid portal by **Benedetto da Maiano**. Designed by **Brunelleschi** and finished, after his death, in 1453, it is one of the more serene spots in Florence.

Museo Nazionale del Bargello

OPEN	Tues-Sat; 2nd and 4th Sun; 1st, 3rd and 5th Mon 8.15-13.50
CLOSED	1st, 3rd and 5th Sun; 2nd and 4th Mon; 1/1, 1/5, 25/12
CHARGES	Full price €4; booking (optional) €1.55 There is a 50% reduction for 18-25-year-olds from the EU and for accredited teachers Admission is free for young people under 18, school groups (participants must be listed on school letterhead), accredited journalists, those accompanying the disabled and EU citizens over 60
TELEPHONE	**055 238 8606**; booking and information **055 294 883**

WWW.	firenzemusei.it
MAIN ENTRANCE	Via del Proconsolo 4
DISABLED ACCESS	Yes (ask at Reception)
GUIDED VISITS	Can be organized by contacting the Education Department of the Curator's Office (T 055 238 8658), or the booking service (T 055 294 883). Audio tours available
SERVICES	Cloakroom, bookshop

Florence's National Museum of Sculpture occupies the former Palazzo del Capitano del Popolo, the city's oldest seat of government. Vasari reports that the original core, dating from 1255, was built following a design by Lapo Tedesco, Arnolfo di Cambio's father and teacher, on a property belonging to the church of the Badia facing the Via del Proconsolo. From the late 13c to 1502 the palace was the official residence of the *podestà*, the magistrate who governed the city and who, by tradition, had to come from another town.

From 1502 to 1574 the palace was the seat of the Council of Justice, after which it was taken over by the chief of police known as the *bargello* and was made into a prison, which remained in use until 1857. Around 1860 interest in the Florence's architectural heritage reawakened interest in the palazzo. A complete restoration ensued and the Bargello finally became a sculpture museum in 1886. Two years later the museum received a generous gift of Gothic and Renaissance artefacts from the French antiquarian, Louis Carrand, followed, in 1894, by a bequest by Costantino Ressman, an ambassador and collector of arms and armour. In 1907, Giulio Franchetti donated his collection of fabrics, with examples dating from the 6c to the 18c.

HIGHLIGHTS

Italian Gothic architecture	Buildings
Michelangelo, *Drunken Bacchus*, *Madonna and Child with the Infant St John*, *David-Apollo*	Michelangelo Room
Giambologna, *Mercury*	
Sculptures by Benvenuto Cellini	

Donatello, marble and bronze *Davids*,   Donatello Room
St George
Ghiberti and Brunelleschi's Reliefs of the
Sacrifice of Isaac **for the Baptistery doors**

Verrocchio, *David*   Verrocchio Room

GROUND FLOOR

MICHELANGELO ROOM This large hall (Room 1) displays works
by the author of the *David* and his contemporaries.

Michelangelo's *Drunken Bacchus* was carved in 1496-7, during
the artist's first Roman sojourn, for Cardinal Raffaello Sansoni
Riario, but it failed to meet with his approval and it was sold to the
banker Iacopo Galli, who kept it in his garden for over 50 years. It
was purchased in 1571 by the Medici and brought to Florence. The
sculpture relies on ancient Roman nude figures as a point of
departure, but it is much more mobile and more complex in
outline. The conscious instability evokes the god of wine and
Dionysiac revels with extraordinary virtuosity. It is also unique
among Michelangelo's works in calling for observation from all
sides rather than primarily from the front.

Michelangelo 'roughed out and did not finish' the *Madonna and
Child with the Infant St John* (*Pitti Tondo*), for Bartolomeo Pitti in
1504-5, while working on the much more exacting *David*. A work
from the artist's youth, the *Pitti Tondo* reveals a progressive
abandonment of distinct outlines and the gradual and subtle
approach to chiaroscuro effects. The forms carry symbolic
references to Christ's future ordeal, common in images of the
Christ Child at the time; they also betray the artist's fascination
with the work of Leonardo. The private nature of the commission
and the domestic devotional role of the piece were such that this
Madonna and Child remained practically unknown until the early
years of the 19c.

The small figure representing *Apollo* or *David* extracting an
arrow from his quiver was carved by Michelangelo in 1530-2. In
the 1568 edition of his *Lives* Vasari mentions that the statue was in

MUSEO NAZIONALE DEL BARGELLO
Second Floor

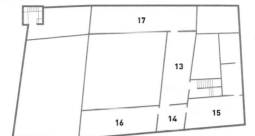

First Floor

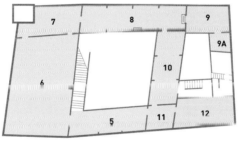

Ground Floor

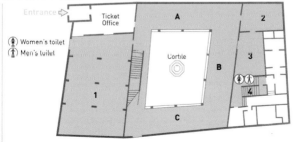

'the hall of the Prince of Florence' remarking that this was 'a most singular occurrence, considering that it is not completely finished'; a contemporary inventory records it in the chambers of Cosimo I at Palazzo Vecchio. Subsequently it was placed in the amphitheatre at Boboli. In 1824 it was transferred to the Uffizi, where it stood opposite the Bacchus; it passed to the Bargello in the 1870s.

The bust of *Brutus* (1539-40) was commissioned from Michelangelo by his friend Cardinal Niccolò Ridolfi through Donato Giannotti, both of whom were exponents of the anti-Medici party. The commission was to commemorate, through the example of Caesar's murderer, the assassination in 1537 of Duke Alexander de' Medici, oppressor of Florentine freedom, by his cousin Lorenzino. Carefully avoiding all political nuance, the pro-Medici Vasari calls the design of the bust purely Classical in inspiration: 'a head of Brutus in marble, with a bust, considerably larger than life size ... performed through the most minute chiselling [and] ... taken from a portrait of Brutus engraved in a very ancient cameo'. The unfinished bust was purchased by Grand Duke Ferdinand I in 1590 and placed in the Uffizi.

The room also holds a marble *Bacchus* sculpted by **Jacopo Sansovino** around 1520; a bronze bust of *Cosimo I* and a number of wax and bronze models for the *Perseus* by **Benvenuto Cellini** (p 17); and **Giambologna**'s *Mercury*, a bronze from 1564.

COURTYARD The Gothic courtyard is adorned with coats of arms of the former *podestà* and, under the colonnade, several fine sculptures: (A) **Benedetto da Maiano**'s high relief of the *Crowning of Ferdinand of Aragon*, with six young musicians and a seated effigy of Alfonso of Aragon attributed to Francesco Laurana, and Niccolò di Pietro Lamberti's *St Luke*, formerly in a niche of Orsanmichele; six beautiful statues by (B) **Ammannati** (1556-63) from an allegorical fountain designed for the Salone dei Cinquecento in Palazzo della Signoria and subsequently set up at the Villa di Pratolino and in the Boboli Gardens; (C) **Giambologna**'s colossal *Oceanus* from Boboli and the magnificent bronze *Cannon of St Paul* from Livorno Castle.

MEDIEVAL SCULPTURE ROOM *Room 2* This room, on the east side of the courtyard, displays sculptural and architectural ornaments from suppressed churches and convents in Florence and its environs. On the back wall is a group of three large statues in *pietra serena* representing the **Madonna and Child between St Peter and St Paul**, by Paolo di Giovanni, made for the gateway of Porta Romana around 1320. The sandstone **Aedicula** and the **Bishop in Benediction**, attributed to Tino di Camaino (or Giovanni di Balduccio) are from the church of Santa Maria Novella.

The adjoining room (3) is used for temporary exhibitions; an internal stair (4) ascends to the first floor, but it is much more exciting to take the beautiful external staircase.

FIRST FLOOR

VERONE *Room 5* Several works by the Flemish-born artist **Giambologna**, one of the pre-eminent Mannerist sculptors who worked in Florence, have been positioned beneath the arches of the airy loggia known as the Verone, constructed between 1317 and 1320. These include personifications of **Architecture** and **Geometry** and a superb collection bronze animals (**Turkey**, **Peacock**, **Lapwing**, **Eagle**, **Eaglet**, **Rooster**, **Owl** and **Barn Owls**) made in 1564-7 for the grotto of the villa Medici at Castello. Among the reliefs on the walls are Baccio Bandinelli's **Drunkenness of Noah**, Francesco Moschino's **Diana and Actaeon**, and various marble medallions that illustrate the Classical flavour of the Grand-ducal collections.

DONATELLO ROOM *Room 6* In 1886 the huge room that was the former Great Council Chamber was used to display the works of **Donatello** and of other Florentine Renaissance sculptors: the works of the master, in chronological order, are the marble *David* produced for the apse of Florence cathedral in 1409, considered one of his earliest sculptures; the *St George* from Orsanmichele (1417); the *Marzocco*, the heraldic lion of the city of Florence, sculpted between 1418 and 1420; the lively polychrome terracotta bust of *Niccolò da Uzzano* (1425-30; also attributed to Desiderio da ase FLORENCE

Settignano); the humorous bronze putto known as *Atys-Amorino*, made after 1430; and the beautiful bronze *David*, executed for Cosimo the Elder around 1440-50.

Also on display in this room are outstanding works by **Desiderio da Settignano** and **Luca della Robbia**, and two panels depicting the *Sacrifice of Isaac* made by **Lorenzo Ghiberti** and **Filippo Brunelleschi** for the competition for the second bronze doors of the baptistery.

Donatello's St George and David

The *St George*, which dominates the room from its reconstructed niche on the north wall, represents a new departure from traditional Gothic sculpture. The *St George* is a perfect blend of the medieval warrior-saint and the Renaissance man of individual initiative. In the relief of *St George Killing the Dragon* (1416–7), under the niche occupied by the statue, Donatello introduced another great innovation; he conceived of a very low relief, known as *schiacciato* ('flattened out'), in which the subtle modelling of planes suggests the illusion of depth and figures moving in space while still respecting the integrity of the plane. He continued to develop the potentialities of this relief style throughout his long career and strongly determined the kind of relief sculpture executed in Florence.

The bronze *David* comes closer to recapturing the spirit of antiquity than any other work of the early Renaissance - indeed, the very idea of a freestanding sculpture of a nude hero was without precedent since antiquity. Well-proportioned and superbly poised, it was conceived independently of any architectural setting. Its harmonious calm makes it the most Classical of Donatello's works.

The marble *David* (in the centre between the windows) is the earliest of Donatello's sculptures housed in the Bargello. Sculpted for the apse of Florence Cathedral, in 1416 it was transferred to the Palazzo della Signoria as a symbol of Florentine freedom. A work of the sculptor's youth, the elegance of the enveloping drapery and the graduated tension of the torso reveal the rhythms of an influence that is still Gothic.

ISLAMIC ART *Room 7* The next room is devoted to works of Islamic art from the old collections of the Medici and Lorraine, and from the modern Carrand, Ressman and Franchetti collections. On display is superb metalwork in bronze, silver and brass, with exceptionally intricate decorative designs, some of them engraved. Highlights include two *Incense Burners* of the 14c-15c, from Syria; a 15c *Persian Vase*; and a *Goblet* engraved and encrusted with gold and silver, made in Cairo for a Yemenite sultan in the Mameluke period (1363-77).

Of exceptional importance are the ivories (*Elephant chess-piece*, Mesopotamia, 9c; six *Plaquettes with Hunting and Court Scenes* from Egypt, 10c-12c), the Persian and Turkish arms (15c-17c), the coloured glass *Mosque-lamp* commissioned by Emir as-Sayfi Tughaytamur an-Nasiri (1342-5); the *Holbein* and *Lotto carpets* (so called after the artists who have depicted them in their paintings); and the textile exhibits, which are shown on a rotating basis for conservation reasons. Among the ceramics worthy of note are the splendid multicoloured Persian and Turkish 'metallic lustre' wall tiles.

SALONE DEL PODESTÀ *Room 8* The Salone del Podestà houses the best examples of Gothic and Renaissance minor arts bequeathed to the Bargello by Louis Carrand. Here are ancient and modern jewellery, including the famous gilt-bronze relief known as *Agylulf's Plate*, a 6c or 7c example of Lombard art discovered by chance near Lucca in 1891; and Limoges enamels, notably a group of gilt-copper engraved champlevé enamel plaques. On the walls are small Italian and Flemish gold-ground paintings, including the famous *Carrand Diptych*, a work of the late-14c Parisian school representing a *Sacra Conversazione* (left panel) and the *Crucifixion* (right).

CAPELLA DEL PODESTÀ *Room 9* The priors' chapel, dedicated to St Mary Magdalene, dates from the early 14c but was subsequently converted to prison cells. The fragmentary frescoes were attributed to Giotto when they were discovered in 1841, on the basis of a popular legend supported by Vasari, but they are now thought to be by his pupils. The scene of *Paradise* on the altar wall includes a portrait of Dante, who appears in the group on the right, dressed in dark red. The triptych of the *Madonna and Child with Saints* was painted by Giovanni di Francesco around 1450. The inlaid-wood choir stalls and lectern come from the abbey of Monteoliveto. Cases in the chapel and the adjacent sacristy (9A) contain silver and gold liturgical objects, mainly from the Carrand collection.

ROOM OF IVORIES *Room 10* Most of the objects here - diptychs, plaquettes, mirror-cases, pastoral staffs, caskets, combs, hunting horns and statuettes - were also bequeathed to the museum in 1888 by Carrand. The use of ivory spread from Byzantium to the court of Charlemagne in the 8c and 9c and was particularly popular in France during the Gothic period. On the walls are polychrome wooden sculptures dating from the 13c to the 15c, 13c-14c paintings of the Tuscan school, and two rare mosaics: a mid-12c *Pantocrator* and *St Peter* from the workshop of Domenico Ghirlandaio (15c).

SALA BRUZZICHELLI *Room 11* This room takes its name from a gift made to the museum in 1983 by the Florentine antiquary Giovanni Bruzzichelli. The outstanding pieces are the two *Cabinets* from the Confraternity of San Michele at Carmignano, the large *Table*, the four large Florentine Renaissance *Stools*, and the small Tuscan *Tabernacle* in gilt and painted wood. On the walls are marble reliefs, mosaics (*Portrait of Pietro Bembo* by Valerio Zuccato), papier-mâché (*Madonna and Child* by Jacopo Sansovino) and wooden sculptures (*Madonna of Mercy*).

MAJOLICA The Bargello's majolica collection owes much to the Medici's passion for collecting, in particular that of Cosimo I, who especially appreciated the art of ceramics and porcelain-making. Thanks to many gifts, also by modern collectors, the majolica room offers a substantially complete panorama of the history of this art in Italy - featuring extremely rare 15c pieces from the Cafaggiolo and Deruta workshops and, from the 16c, important examples of Urbino and Faenza majolica, as well as splendid examples of Venetian ware.

SECOND FLOOR

DELLA ROBBIA ROOMS *Rooms 13, 14* Two whole rooms are dedicated to the glazed terracotta works of **Giovanni** and **Andrea della Robbia**. Giovanni was the son of Andrea della Robbia and grandnephew of Luca della Robbia; he assumed control of the family workshop upon the death of his father in 1525. His creations are distinguished by the use of a wide range of colours, narrative variety, and rich detail and decoration. The outstanding pieces exhibited in this room include the *Adoration of the Magi*, a work of the artist's youth; and the *Pietà* of 1514 with its lively polychrome background and predella with an *Annunciation* flanked by putti in swaddling clothes.

Andrea was the nephew of Luca della Robbia and took over the family workshop after his uncle's death in 1482. He was acquainted with the foremost painters and architects of his time, and this fact, along with the commissions from members of the Medici circle and the Franciscan and Dominican monastic orders, made his reputation throughout Europe. The descriptive pictorial tones of his early Madonnas developed into the serene and tender portrayals typified by the *Madonna of the Architects* (1475), the *Madonna of the Cushion* from the convent of the Badia, or the tondo of the *Madonna and Child*. In the centre of the room is the intimate little *Portrait of a Boy* (c 1474), possibly Pietro di Lorenzo de'Medici.

VERROCCHIO ROOM *Room 15* This room houses Tuscan works from the second half of the 15c; the best represented artist is clearly the 'Florentine ... goldsmith, master of perspective, sculptor, engraver, painter and musician' (Vasari) and, one should add, master of Leonardo da Vinci, Andrea del Verrocchio.

Dominating the centre of the room is Verrocchio's famous bronze *David*. This statue was commissioned by the Medici family and it was sold by them in 1476 to the Signoria, the ruling body of Florence, and placed in the Palazzo Vecchio, thus gaining a republican meaning similar to Donatello's *David*. The explicitness and angularity of Verrocchio's figure contrast with the ambiguity and sensuousness of Donatello's, nude and vulnerable where Verrocchio's is elegantly clothed. Verrocchio's *David* carries a small sword in one hand and, with his other confidently poised on his hip, looks triumphantly out at the viewer. The figure, to be viewed in the round, lacks the anatomical exaggerations and the psychological implications or complexity of Donatello's. It is, rather, perfectly chased and was meant to be appreciated for its exquisite patina.

The idealization of the individual that characterizes Verrocchio's marble bust known as the *Noblewoman with Bouquet* (1475-80) created a new type of Renaissance portrait sculpture, in which the arms of the sitter are included in the manner of ancient Roman models. This compositional device allows the hands, as well as the face, to express the character and mood of the sitter. The innovation was not lost on Verrocchio's pupil, Leonardo da Vinci, who would exploit its potential in his painted portraits. Indeed the sitter of this bust has sometimes been identified as Ginevra dei Benci, the subject of a Leonardo portrait. However, it is generally assumed she is Lucrezia Donati, a platonic love of Lorenzo il Magnifico.

The only known example of the wooden crucifixes made by Verrocchio and recorded by Vasari, the painted *Crucifix* of 1480, comes from the Confraternity of St Francis in Piazza Santissima Annunziata. A distinctive chromatic softness lends the sculpture a pathos and an emotional quality that became characteristic of the artist's later work. It provides an exceptional example of the direct relationship Verrocchio sought to establish between sculptural and pictorial language, or rather the combination and subtle blending of the two.

Also in the room are portraits by other prominent 15c artists, among them *Piero Mellini* by **Benedetto da Maiano** (signed and dated 1474); *Matteo Palmieri* (signed and dated 1478) and *Francesco Sassetti* (both by **Antonio Rossellino**); *Piero de' Medici, Rinaldo della Luna* and *Giovanni de' Medici* by Mino da Fiesole, and

Battista Sforza, wife of Federico da Montefeltro, by Francesco Laurana.

SALA DEL CAMINO *Room 16* This room, which takes its name from the magnificent chimneypiece at the far end (by Benedetto da Rovezzano; firedogs by Niccolò Roccatagliata), contains the Bargello's splendid collection of **small bronzes**. The objects vary widely in size, shape and subject, but they all share a common characteristic: the blending of artistic ingenuity with extraordinary casting techniques. Included are pieces from the Medici collections as well as works bequeathed in 1888 by Louis Carrand. One of the more memorable is **Antonio Pollaiolo**'s *Hercules and Antaeus* (c 1478), a forceful depiction of the struggle between these two powerful men from Classical mythology. The angular contours of the limbs and the jagged voids between the figures are all directed toward expressing tautness and muscular strain. Of Pollaiolo Vasari wrote in his *Lives*. 'He understood the nude in a more modern sense than other masters before him, and he dissected many bodies to observe their underlying anatomy.'

ARMOURY *Room 17* The armoury has a splendid display of ceremonial arms and armour - cross-bows, sabres, rapiers, shields and calvary armour, breastplates, daggers, halberds, and a fine collection of historic firearms - from the Medici collections and Carrand and Ressmann bequests. Highlights include the gold-trimmed Roman-style breastplate made by Filippo Negroli around 1546, for Cosimo I's nomination as Knight of the Golden Fleece; and two helmets made for the ceremonial game of *borgognotta*: one with an eagle crest, the other with a design of foliage and grotesques.

THE MEDAGLIERE MEDICEO *Rooms 18, 19* exhibit a vast number of comemmorative medals in chronological order - **Pisanello**'s medallion of *Lionello d'Este*, Marquis of Ferrara, c 1440, and Niccolò Fiorentino's *Giovanna Albizzi*, 1485-6, made for her marriage with Lorenzo Tornabuoni are outstanding examples - together with Baroque sculpture. At the centre of the first room is

Gianlorenzo Bernini's marble *Bust of Costanza Bonarelli* (1636), whose slightly disordered garments and hair, sensuous full features and robust neck recall the paintings of Rubens; and an unfinished bust of *Cardinal Paolo Emilio Wacchia Rondanini* by Alessandro Algardi (c 1650).

on route

Badia Fiorentina, Via del Proconsolo. Open Mon 15.00-16.00. The Badia is the church of a Benedictine abbey founded in 978 by Willa, widow of Uberto, Margrave of Tuscany. It was enlarged in the 13c and redesigned in the early 17c. Dante tells that he saw Beatrice at Mass here and that the bells of the Badia gave the medieval city the hours. To the left of the entrance is Filippino Lippi's masterpiece of the *Madonna Appearing to St Bernard* (c 1485). The large 15c cloister was designed by Bernardo Rossellino.

Casa Buonarroti, Via Ghibellina 70. Open daily except Tues 9.30-14.00. Full price €6.50; €4 for under 18 and over 60, *T* 055 241 752. The Casa Buonarroti was purchased in 1508 by Michelangelo, whose descendants lived here and turned part of it into a memorial to him. Many of the rooms were decorated by the artist's great-nephew, Michelangelo Buonarroti il Giovani (1568-1646).

The important works by the sculptor, on the first floor, include a bas-relief known as the *Madonna of the Steps*, his earliest known work (c 1490), showing the influence of Donatello's *schaicciato* relief style; the *Battle of the Centaurs* (1490-2), a superb anatomical study made when Michelangelo was just 16; and a stunning large-scale study for the torso of a *River God* (c 1524-7), the only sculpture Michelangelo shaped directly with his hands (the others are all carved with hammer and chisel). There is also a superb collection of more than 200 drawings, shown on a rotating basis for reasons of conservation.

Museo Horne, Via dei Benci 6. Open daily except Sun 9.00-13.00. Full price €5; €3 for under 18 and over 65. *T* 055 244 661. The two enduring achievements of the English art historian Herbert Percy Horne (1864-1916) were his pioneering work on Botticelli, then still an undervalued artist, and the collection of 14c-16c paintings, sculpture and decorative arts he installed in this palace where he lived during the last few years of his life.

Museo Nazionale di Antropologia ed Etnologia, Via del Proconsolo. Open daily except Tues 9.00-13.00. Full price €4, *T* 055 239 6449. Italy's most important ethnological and anthropological collections occupy 35 rooms in the imposing Palazzo Nonfinito.

commercial galleries

Santo Ficara, Via Ghibellina 164r, *T* 055 234 0239. Italian artists of international standing: Carla Accardi, Giuseppe Chiari, Luigi Mainolfi, Aldo Mondino and others.

eating and drinking

Like the Oltrano, Santa Croce is a bohemian neighbourhood, traditionally home to the city's poor labouring class and now a good place to go for food, drink and nightlife. Here you will find the city's most expensive restaurant (Enoteca Pinchiorri) as well as several of the cheapest - and all are good.

RESTAURANTS

€   **Baraonda**, Via Ghibellina 67r, *T* 055 234 1171; closed Sunday and midday Monday. Elegant *trattoria* with traditional Tuscan cuisine and good service.

Danny Rock, Via Pandolfini 13r, *T* 055 235 0307; closed two weeks in August. Hot student joint, serving hamburgers, pizza and sweet and savoury crêpes.

I Ghibellini, Piazza San Piero Maggiore 8-10r, *T* 055 214 424; closed Wednesday. Pizza and simple Tuscan dishes.

Pallottino, Via Isola delle Stinche 1r, *T* 055 289 573; closed Monday and in August. Well-known *trattoria* offering creative interpretations of Tuscan recipes.

La Raccolta, Via Leopardi 2r, *T* 055 247 9086; open midday only. Delicious organic food.

Le Campane, Borgo la Croce 87r, *T* 055 234 1101; always open. Good pizza and creative Tuscan cooking, somewhat lacking in atmosphere.

Ruth's, Via Farini 2, *T* 055 248 0888; closed Friday evening, midday Saturday and Jewish holidays. Fine Mediterranean Kosher cuisine in a small, lively environment. No credit cards.

Sedeno Allegro, Borgo la Croce 20r, *T* 055 234 5505; closed Wednesday. Fine vegetarian food, pleasant atmosphere.

€€ **Acqua al**, 2 Via della Vigna Vecchia 40r, *T* 055 284 170; closed one week in August. Good, simple and affordable Tuscan fare; crowded with Florentines.

Da Benvenuto, Via della Mosca 16r, *T* 055 214 833; closed Sunday. A simple *trattoria* much loved by Florentines.

Da Carmine-Il Pizzaiuolo, Via De'Macci 113r, *T* 055 241 171; closed in August and late December-early January. Neapolitan cuisine, including delicious pizza. No credit cards.

Del Fagioli, Corso Tintori 47r, *T* 055 244 285; closed Saturday, Sunday and in August. Typical Tuscan *trattoria*. No credit cards.

l' cché c'è c'è, Via Magalotti 11r, *T* 055 216 589; closed Monday. Creative interpretations of traditional Tuscan recipes in a friendly atmosphere.

€€€ **Alle Murate**, Via Ghibellina 52r, *T* 055 240 618; closed midday, all day Monday and two weeks in December. Elegant and romantic, with great innovative interpretations of traditional recipes, and a fabulous wine list.

Cibreo, Via de'Macci 114, *T* 055 234 1100; closed Sunday, Monday and in late July-early August. This one comes in two sizes, depending on your budget. The front door brings you into the roomy *ristorante*, where the spoken menu is rich and varied and the prices, on the high side. The back door opens onto the tiny *osteria*, where you can enjoy a limited menu for almost half the money. In both places, you'll get a memorable meal, including vegetarian dishes. No credit cards.

Enoteca Pinchiorri, Via Ghibellina 87, *T* 055 242 777; closed Sunday, Monday and midday Tuesday; August, late December–early January. Florence's most elegant restaurant, serving innovative interpretations of traditional Tuscan cuisine and fine wines in a 16c building.

WINE BARS

€   **Italianloves**, Via dei Pepi 4-6r. Wine bar, wine shop and internet point all rolled into one.

   Vini, Via dell'Anguillara 70r, no *T*, closed Sunday. A drive-thru for walkers.

€€   **Baldovino**, Via San Giuseppe 18r, *T* 055 234 7220; closed Monday. Friendly and refined, opposite the north flank of the church of Santa Croce, with good *crostini*, sandwiches, cheeses and great wines.

   Balducci, Via de' Neri 2r, *T* 055 216 887; closed Monday and late July–early August. Its *bruschette* and pasta dishes draw quite a crowd at lunchtime.

   Enoteca Boccadama, Piazza Santa Croce 25-26r, *T* 055 243 640; closed Saturday evening (Monday in winter). A classic *enoteca* offering hundreds of Italian and foreign wines, plus simple but delicious warm and cold meals, right on one of the city's most frequented squares.

   Enoteca de' Giraldi, Via de' Giraldi 4r, *T* 055 216 518; closed Sunday and holidays. A little hard to find (Via de' Giraldi is a cross-street of Via Pandolfini and Borgo degli Albizi), this pleasant place specializes in lesser-known Tuscan wines, excellent salads and delicious cheeses.

   Osteria del Caffè Italiano, Via Isola delle Stinche 11r, *T* 055 289 368; closed Monday, in August and December. The excellent wine bar is by the entrance; the restaurant beyond is less interesting.

CAFÉS

€   **Dolci e Dolcezze**, Piazza Beccaria 8r. You haven't seen chocolate until you've been here.

   Vivoli, Via Isola delle Stinche 7r. Florence's most famous ice cream, popular with the student crowd.

shopping

Walking through Santa Croce you will see plenty of shops selling leather goods: they are for tourists only and the best deals are elsewhere. Bargain hunters will especially enjoy the Mercats delle Parli and the colourful grocery market at Sant' Ambrogio.

ANTIQUES

Mercato delle Pulci (flea market), Piazza dei Ciompi. A good place to find small antiques and craft items. Closed Sunday and Monday in winter.

BOOKS

Paperback Exchange, Via Fiesolana 31r. New and used books in Italian, English and other major languages; you can trade in the dull one you're reading and use the credit towards something more exciting.

FOOD

Dolci e Dolcezze, Piazza Beccaria 8r. You haven't seen chocolate until you've been here; also a café.

La Raccolta, Via Leopardi 2r. Organic foods, including fresh baked goods.

Mercato di Sant'Ambrogio, Piazza Sant'Ambrogio. A pocket-size version of the Mercato Centrale, selling foods of all kinds - fruit and vegetables outside, meats, cheeses, pasta, etc, inside.

THE HOME

Andreini, Borgo degli Albizi 63. Ceramics for the home.

Ceramica Artistica Migliori, Via dei Benci 39. Contemporary copies of antique Italian majolica.

Coltelleria Fiorentina, Via dei Neri 63. Beautiful cutlery.

Sbigoli, Via Sant'Egidio 4. A wide selection of traditional Tuscan ceramics.

JEWELLERY

Messico e Nuvole, Borgo degli Albizi 54r, *T* 055 242 677.

entertainment

INFORMATION
TICKETS
THEATRE AND CINEMA
MUSIC
SPECIAL EVENTS

INFORMATION

For information on concerts, theatre, live music cafés, etc, consult
Firenze Spettacolo, a monthly magazine sold at newsstands, or
Vista magazine, which has monthly listings in English.

TICKETS

Box Office, Via Alamanni 39, *T* 055 210 804; Via Porta Rossa 82r,
T 055 219 402; Viale Gianotti 13/15, *T* 055 680 362; Via Vittorio Emanuele
303; *T* 055 422 0361; www.boxoffice.it, firenze@boxoffice.it, provides
advance booking and ticket sales for many events.

THEATRE AND CINEMA

British Institute, Lungarno Guicciardini 9, *T* 055 267 78270. Films in
English every Wednesday.

Cinema Fulgor, Via Maso Finiguerra 22r, *T* 055 238 1881,
www.cinemafulgor.it. Original language films every Thursday.

Deutsches Institut, Via Orti Oricellari 10, *T* 055 215 993,
www.deutschesinstitut.it. German-language films.

Institut Français de Florence, Piazza Ognissanti 2, *T* 055 239 8902,
www.istitutofrancese.it, france-m@fol.it. Movies in French.

Teatro della Limonaia, Via Gramsci 462, Sesto Fiorentino, *T* 055 440 852,
www.teatro-limonaia.fi.it, info@teatro-limonaia.fi.it. New Italian and
international drama; Intercity Festival.

Teatro della Pergola, Via della Pergola 12/32, *T* 055 22641,
www.pergola.firenze.it, ufficio.promozione@pergola.firenze.it.
Mainstream theatre, from Molière to the Moderns.

Teatro Puccini, Piazza Puccini, *T* 055 362 067, www.teatropuccini.it; info@teatropuccini.it. Fringe theatre.

Teatro Studio di Scandicci, Via Donizetti 58, Scandicci, *T* 055 757 348, www.scandiccicultura.org, teatrostudio@scandiccicultura.org. Experimental theatre.

Teatro Verdi, Via Ghibellina 99, *T* 055 212 320, www.teatroverdi firenze.it, info@teatroverdifirenze.it. Theatre season.

MUSIC

OPERA, BALLET AND CLASSICAL
Accademia Bartolomeo Cristofori Amici del Fortepiano, Via Camaldoli 7, *T* 055 221646. Classical concert series.

Conservatorio Statale di Musica, Luigi Cherubini, Via delle Belle Arti 2, *T* 055 210 502, 055 292 180. Classical concert series.

Cattedrale di Santa Maria del Fiore, Piazza Duomo, *T* 055 230 2885, www.operaduomo.firenze.it. *O Flos Colende* religious music series in the Duomo.

Istituto Francese, Piazza Ognissanti 2, *T* 055 239 8902, www. istitutofrancese.it. *Europamusica* classical music series.

Orchestra da Camera Fiorentina, Via Poggi 6, *T* 055 783 374, www.orcafi.it. Chamber music series in the church of Santo Stefano al Ponte Vecchio, Via Por Santa Maria.

Teatro Comunale/Maggio Musicale Fiorentino, Corso Italia 16, *T* 800 112 211, www.maggiofiorentino.com, tickets@maggiofiorentino.com. Opera, concerts, ballet and *Maggio Musicale Fiorentino* classical music season.

Teatro della Pergola, Via della Pergola 12/32, *T* 055 22641, www.pergola.firenze.it, ufficio.promozione@pergola.firenze.it. *Amici della Musica* classical concert series.

Teatro Verdi, Via Ghibellina 99, *T* 055 212 320, www.teatroverdi firenze.it, info@teatroverdifirenze.it. Classical concert season.

JAZZ/ROCK
Astor Caffè, Piazza Duomo 20r. Live hip-hop, soul and rhythm 'n' blues.

Auditorium Flog, Via Mercati 24b, *T* 055 240 397, www.flog.it. Jazz, rock and pop concert series.

Bizzeffe, Via Panicale 61r, *T* 055 274 1009, www.bzf.it. Jazz concert series.

Caffè La Torre, Lungarno Benvenuto Cellini 65r, *T* 055 680 643. Jazz concert series.

H2O2, Via Pandolfini 26r, *T* 055 243 356. Live rock music.

Hotel Excelsior, Piazza Ognissanti 3, *T* 055 264 201. Sunday brunch jazz concert series.

Jazz Club, Via Nuova de' Caccini 3, *T* 055 247 9700. Jazz, swing and blues concert series.

Musicus Concentus, Piazza del Carmine 14, *T* 055 287 347, www.musicusconcentus.com. Jazz concert series at the Sala Vanni, Santa Maria del Carmine.

Palasport, Via Pasquale Paoli, *T* 055 678 841. Large rock concerts.

Pinocchio, Viale Giannotti 13, *T* 055 683 388. Jazz concert series.

Saschall Lungarno, Aldo Moro *T* 055 650 4112, www.saschall.it. Tented theatre and concert hall.

Teatro Puccini, Via delle Cascine 41, *T* 055 362 067, www.teatro puccini.it. Jazz concert series, as well as cinema and theatre.

Teatro Verdi, Via Ghibellina 99, *T* 055 212 320, www.teatroverdi firenze.it, info@teatroverdifirenze.it. Pop concert series.

Tenax, Via Pratese 46, *T* 055 552 0575, www.tenax.org. Rock and pop concert series

XO, Via Giuseppe Verdi 57r, *T* 055 234 1529. Live rock music.

SPECIAL EVENTS

Calcio Storico, Piazza Santa Croce. The historic football game played here probably has roots in the *arpasto* played by Roman legionnaires in the ancient *Florentia* - some of the schemes of play resemble Roman battle manoeuvres. During the republican period young people of good lineage and special physical strength were chosen to represent the neighbourhood militias, as a means of keeping espril de corps high. Today the neighbourhoods' roughest, toughest youths dress in colourful costume and match muscle in a purpose-built temporary arena. Finals on 24 June.

Festa della Rificolona. The Virgin's birthday (8 September) is celebrated the previous evening by children carrying paper lanterns through the streets, especially in Piazza Santissima Annunziata and along the Arno; other kids with pea-shooters try to smash the lanterns.

Festa di San Giovanni, Piazzale Michelangelo. The feast of Florence's patron saint is celebrated with a massive fireworks display beginning at dusk, 24 June.

Firenze Marathon, Piazzale Michelangelo. International marathon and half marathon, run in November.

Mostra Internazionale dell'Artigianato Fortezza da Basso. International Handicraft Exhibition with exhibitors from around the world and annual monographic themes; April-May.

Mostra-Mercato di Piante e Fiori Giardino dell'Orticultura. Plant and flower show sponsored by the Società Italiana di Orticoltura; spring and autumn.

Scopio del Carro Piazza del Duomo. Half pagan, half Christian, this is the first major folk festival of the year. A cartload of fireworks is hauled by six white oxen from the Porta a Prato to the cathedral; here, the whole lot is set off by a 'dove' that whizzes down a wire from the high altar. Easter Day.

planning

TOURIST OFFICES
GETTING THERE
GETTING AROUND
INFORMATION OFFICES
OTHER ESSENTIALS
PLACES TO STAY

TOURIST OFFICES ABROAD

CANADA
Italian Government Tourist Board, 175 Bloor Street E., Suite 907 – South Tower, M4W 3R8 Toronto (Ontario), *T* 416 925 4882, *F* 416 925 4799, www.italiantourism.com, enit.canada@on.aibn.com

UK AND IRELAND
Italian State Tourist Board, 1 Princes Street, London W1R 7RA, *T* 020 7408 1254, *F* 020 7493 6695, www.enit.il, italy@italiantouristboard.co.uk

USA
Italian Government Tourist Board, 630 Fifth Avenue, Suite 1565, New York, NY 10111, *T* 212 245 4822, *F* 212 586 9249, www.italiantourism.com, enitny@italiantourism.com

500 North Michigan Avenue, Suite 2240, Chicago 1, IL 60611, *T* 312 644 0996, *F* 312 644 3019, www.italiantourism.com, enitch@italiantourism.com

12400 Wilshire Blvd, Suite 550, Los Angeles, CA 90025, *T* 310 820 1898, *F* 310 820 6357, www.italiantourism.com, enitla@ italiantourism.com

ONLINE
The official website of the Florence tourist office (Agenzia per il Turismo a Firenze) is: www.firenzeturismo.it

INFORMATION OFFICES IN FLORENCE

Agenzia per la Promozione Turistica di Firenze, Via Manzoni 16,
T 055 23320, *F* 055 234 6286, info@firenze.turismo.toscana.it

Ufficio Informazioni Turistiche, APT Via Cavour 1r, *T* 055 290 832/3,
F 055 2760383, infoturismo@provincia.fi.it

Ufficio Informazioni Turistiche del Comune di Firenze, Piazza Stazione 4a,
T 055 212 245, *F* 055 238 1226, turismo3@comune.fi.it

Ufficio Informazioni Turistiche del Comune di Firenze, Borgo Santa Croce
29r, *T* 055 234 0444, *F* 055 226 4524

Ufficio Informazioni Turistiche, APT Aeroporto Firenze Via del Termine 1,
Peretola *T/F* 055 315 874, infoaeroporto@aeroporto. firenze.it

GETTING THERE
BY AIR

Florence is served by two regional airports handling domestic and
European flights. Florence's Aeroporto Amerigo Vespucci, just a
few kilometres west of the city, is the most convenient; the
Aeroporto Galileo Galilei is at Pisa, 85km west. Direct flights
operate throughout the year from London Stansted and Gatwick to
one or both of these. There are also flights from Australia, Britain,
Ireland and North America to the major continental European
airports, from which regional flights connect to Florence.

Aeroporto Amerigo Vespucci, *T* 055 315 874 or 055 373 498

Aeroporto Galileo Galilei, *T* 050 500 707

FROM THE UK
Alitalia, *T* 0870 544 8259, www.alitalia.co.uk

British Airways, *T* 0870 850 9850, www.ba.com

Bmibaby, *T* 0870 264 2229, www.bmibaby.com

easyJet, *T* 0871 7500 100, www.easyjet.com

Meridiana, *T* 020 7839 2222, www.meridiana.it

Ryanair, *T* 0905 566 0000, www.ryanair.com

REPUBLIC OF IRELAND
Aer Lingus, *T* 0818 365 000, www.aerlingus.com

Alitalia, *T* 01 677 5171, www.alitalia.co.uk

FROM THE USA AND CANADA
AeroMexico, *T* 1 800 237 6639, www.aeromexico.com, from Atlanta, Miami, New York to Milan; from Atlanta and New York to Rome

Air Canada, *T* 1 888 247 2262, from the USA 1 800 268 0024, www.aircanada.ca, from Toronto to Milan and Rome

Alitalia, *T* 1 800 223 5730, www.alitaliausa.com, from Atlanta, Boston, Chicago, Miami, Toronto to Milan; from New York, Toronto to Rome

Continental, *T* 1 800 525 0280, www.continental.com, from Atlanta, New York to Milan

Delta, *T* 1 800 221 1212, from Atlanta, Boston, Chicago, Miami, New York, to Milan; from Atlanta and New York to Rome; from New York to Venice

United, *T* 1 800 864 8331, www.ual.com, from Washington to Milan

USAir, *T* 1 800 245 4882, from Philadelphia to Rome

Air France (*T* 1 800 237 2747, www.airfrance.com), **British Airways** (*T* 1 800 247 9297, www.britishairways.com), **Brussels Airlines** (*T* 0870 735 2345, www.brusselsairlines.com), **KLM** (*T* 1 800 374 7747); **Lufthansa** (*T* 1 800 645 3880, www.lufthansa.com), and **Swiss Airlines** (*T* 1 877 359 7947, www.swiss.com) offer connecting flights via Paris, London, Brussels, Amsterdam, Frankfurt or Munich and Zurich which are often more economical than the direct flights.

GETTING TO THE CITY CENTRE FROM THE AIRPORTS
From Florence Airport Shuttle buses run every 30mins from the arrivals terminal at Florence Airport to the SITA bus station next to the Santa Maria Novella railway station. The journey takes 20-30mins and tickets (€3.50) can be bought on board. Taxis are usually available at the terminal exit (otherwise *T* 055 4390 or 055 4798).

From Pisa Airport Trains connect Pisa Airport to Florence Santa Maria Novella Station. Trains leave from platforms just outside the terminal; tickets must be bought at the office on your right as you exit the baggage claim area. The journey takes 1hr, and several stops are made on the way. For return flights from Pisa there is an air terminal at Santa Maria Novella station in Florence (on platform 5, open 6.00-16.30), where luggage can be checked and boarding cards obtained for most flights. In summer there is an express coach service between the airport and Florence, which also takes about 1hr.

BY TRAIN
FROM THE UK
European Rail Travel, *T* 020 7387 0444, *F* 020 7387 0888, www.raileurope.co.uk. Information and tickets on the Italian Railways (Trenitalia).

Trenitalia Help Desk, *T* +39 06 8833 9537, *F* +39 06 8833 9613, www.trenitalia.it, helpdesk@sipax.com. Information and tickets with station pick-up in Italy.

FROM THE USA AND CANADA
European Rail Travel, *T* 1 877 257 2887 in the US, *T* 1 800 361 RAIL in Canada, or www.raileurope. com. Information and tickets on the Italian Railways (Trenitalia).

Trenitalia Help Desk, *T* +39 06 8833 9537, *F* +39 06 8833 9613, www. trenitalia.it, helpdesk@sipax.com Information and tickets with station pick-up in Italy,

GETTING AROUND
BY BUS
The orange ATAF and LI-NEA buses are a quick way of travelling around Florence, and relatively easy as bus routes are displayed at bus stops and inside the buses. Most bus stops are request stops (*fermata a richiesta*), and each is indicated by its name on the stop itself. Although buses provide the best means of transport in Florence, now that the city centre has been closed to private traffic they tend to be crowded and it is usually worthwhile walking instead of waiting for a bus.

ATAF runs the town bus service and has an information office under the bus shelter on the east (right) side of the Santa Maria Novella railway station. Open daily 7.00-20.00. For information, *T* 800 424 500 (daily 7.00-20.00) or consult the website www.ataf.net.

TICKETS AND PASSES
All forms of travel pass and ticket (described below) will cover any journey on the Florence bus network. Tickets and bus passes can be purchased at the ATAF offices in Piazza Stazione, or at bars, newsstands, and tobacconists. Tickets must be stamped on the machines on board.

At night, from 21.00 to 6.00, tickets can be purchased aboard from the driver at €2.00.

Fares 60min €1; 3hrs €1.80; daily ticket €4; 2 days €5.70; 3 days €7.20; weekly ticket €12, multi ride (4x60 minutes) €3.90

USEFUL BUS LINES

7 Stazione - S. Domenico - Fiesole

10 Stazione - Campo Marte - Settignano

12/13 Stazione - Piazzale Michelangelo (Camping Michelangelo)

17 Via Verga - Salviatino (Youth Hostel)

25a Stazione - Piazza Libertà - Pratolino

2 Stazione - Sesto Fiorentino - Calenzano (Camping Autosole)

37 Stazione - Porta Romana - Galluzzo (Camping Internazionale Firenze) - Tavarnuzze

BY TAXI

These are hired from ranks or by telephone; there are no cruising cabs. Fares are generally cheaper than in London, though considerably more expensive than in New York. No tip is expected. Supplements are charged for late-night journeys and for luggage. There is a heavy surcharge when the destination is outside the town limits (ask roughly how much the fare is likely to be).

Taxis T 055 4390, 055 4499, 055 4798, 055 4242

BY CAR

It's not a good idea to use your own car in Florence. The city centre is closed to circulation (except for residents) Mon-Sat 7.30-19.30. Access is allowed to hotels and for the disabled. It is always advisable to leave your car in a supervised car park. Always lock your car when parked, and never leave anything of value inside.

BY BICYCLE

The city of Florence rents bicycles (€1.50/hr) throughout the year (8.15-19.30), except Sunday and holidays, from the car parks at the Fortezza da Basso, the Parterre (Piazza della Libertà), Piazza

Vittorio Veneto, Piazza del Cestello, Piazza Torquato Tasso, the Mercato Centrale, Viale Matteotti, Piazza Beccaria, Piazza Piave, Piazza Poggi and the bike stands in Via della Ninna, Piazza Strozzi and Piazza della Stazione. The service is suspended from 1-15 January and 6-27 August. You have to leave a valid document and return the bike before 19.30 to the place from which you hired it.

Firenze Parcheggi at the Parterre car park (Piazza della Libertà), *T* 055 500 9941, www.firenzeparcheggi.it. For information on the city of Florence bicycle hire scheme.

Alinari, Via Guelfa 85r, *T* 055 280 500, www.alinari rental.com. Privately run, with mountain bikes.

Florence by Bike, Via S.Zanobi 120-122r , *T/F* 055 488 992, www.florencebybike.it, ecologica@dada.it. Another private hire firm.

OTHER ESSENTIALS
BANKING SERVICES

The best way to obtain Euros while in Italy is to use a cashpoint card or credit card: in most cities ATM are open 24hrs a day, require no waiting and offer the best exchange rates.

Banks are open Monday-Friday, 8.30-13.30, 14.30-16.00 and are closed on Saturday, Sunday and public holidays. The afternoon opening may vary from bank to bank, and many banks close early (about 11.00) on days preceding national holidays.

CONSULATES

United Kingdom, Lungarno Corsini 2, *T* 055 284 133, *F* 055 219 112; Mon-Fri 9.30-12.30, 14.30-16.30.

United States, Lungarno A. Vespucci 38, *T* 055 239 8276, *F* 055 284 088; Mon-Fri 9.00-12.30, 14-15.30.

The embassies are in Rome.

DISABLED TRAVELLERS

All new public buildings are now obliged by law to provide easy access and specially designed facilities for the disabled. Unfortunately the conversion of historical buildings, including many museums and monuments, is made problematic by structural impediments such as narrow pavements. Barriers therefore continue to exist in many cases. Hotels that are equipped to accommodate the disabled are indicated in the annual list of hotels published by the tourist board. Airports and railway stations provide assistance and certain trains are equipped to transport wheelchairs. Cars with disabled drivers or passengers are allowed access to the centre of town (normally closed to traffic), where special parking places are reserved for them.

HEALTH AND MEDICAL SERVICES

EMERGENCY ROOMS

Policlinico di Careggi, Viale Morgagni 85, *T* 055 427 7111

Ospedale S. Maria Nuova, Piazza S. Maria Nuova 1, *T* 055 27581

Centro Traumatologico Ortopedico (CTO), Largo Palagi 1, *T* 055 427 7111

Istituto Ortopedico Toscano (IOT), Viale Michelangelo 41, *I* 055 65771

Meyer Children's Hospital, Via L. Giordano 13, *T* 055 56621

Nuovo Ospedale S. Giovanni di Dio, Via Torregalli 3, *T* 055 71921

Ospedale S. Maria Annunziata, Via dell'Antella 58, *T* 055 24961

DOCTORS

Arciconfraternità della Misericordia di Firenze, Vicolo degli Adimari 1 (Piazza Duomo) *T* 055 212 221; fee-paying service €23.50, Mar-Oct, Mon-Fri 14.00-18.00.

24 hour Medical Service, Via Lorenzo il Magnifico 59, *T* 055 475 411, *F* 055 474 983, medserv@tin.it; fee-paying service Mon-Fri 11.00-12.00 and 17.00-18.00; English, German and French speaking practitioners and specialists on call 24 hrs.

LATE-NIGHT PHARMACIES

All'Insegna del Moro, Piazza San Giovanni 20r, *T* 055 211 343

Di Rifredi, Piazza Dalmazia 24r, *T* 055 422 0422

Farmacia Comunale no. 13, Stazione Santa Maria Novella, *T* 055 289 435 or 055 216 761

Molteni, Via dei Calzaiuoli 7r, *T* 055 289 490

Paglicci, Via della Scala 61, *T* 055 215 612

INTERNET CENTRES

Internet Train, Via Guelfa 24a; Via dell'Oriuolo 25r; Borgo San Jacopo 30r; Stazione di Santa Maria Novella; Borgo La Croce 33r; Via de' Benci 30r; Via del Parione (Palazzo Corsini); Via Zannoni 1r; Via Porta Rossa 38r; Piazza Duomo 20r (Astor Caffè).

OPENING TIMES

GALLERIES, MUSEUMS AND CHURCHES

The opening times of museums and monuments have been given in the text, but they often change without warning. The tourist board keeps updated timetables of most museums. National museums and monuments are usually open daily 8.15-18.50, plus evening hours in summer. Churches open quite early in the morning (often for 6.00 Mass), but are normally closed for a considerable period during the middle of the day (12.00 or 12.30 to 15.00, 16.00, or 17.00). Some churches ask that sightseers do not enter during a service, but normally visitors may do so, provided they are silent and do not approach the altar in use. In Holy Week most of the pictures are covered and are on no account shown.

SHOPS

Shops generally open Mon-Sat 8.30/9.00-13.00 and 15.30/16.00-19.30/20.00. Shops selling clothes and other goods are usually closed on Monday morning, food shops on Wednesday afternoon, except from mid-June to mid-September, when all shops are closed instead on Saturday afternoon.

PUBLIC HOLIDAYS

1 January
25 April (Liberation Day)
Easter Sunday and Easter Monday
1 May (Labour Day)
24 June (St John the Baptist, patron saint)
15 August (Assumption)
1 November (All Saints' Day)
8 December (Immaculate Conception)
25 December (Christmas Day)
26 December (St Stephen)

SALES TAX REBATES

If you're a non-EU resident, you can claim sales tax rebates on purchases made in Italy provided the total expenditure is more than €150. Ask the vendor for a receipt describing the goods acquired and send it back to him when you get home (but no later than 90 days after the date of the receipt). The receipt must be checked and stamped by Italian customs on leaving Italy. On receipt of the bill, the vendor will forward the sales tax rebate (the present tax rate is 20 per cent on most goods) to your home address.

USEFUL TELEPHONE NUMBERS

AT&T operator, *T* 800 246 748.

Directory assistance, *T* 12 (for numbers in Italy), *T* 176 (for international numbers).

For a wake-up call, *T* 114 and follow the prompts (in Italian).

TIPPING

A service charge of 15 to 18 per cent is added to hotel bills. The service charge is already included when all-inclusive prices are quoted, but it is customary to leave an additional tip in any case. As a guideline and depending on the category of your hotel, a tip of €1-2 is suggested for hotel staff except the concierge who may expect a little more (€2-3).

Restaurants add a service charge of approximately 15 per cent to all bills. It is customary, however, to leave a small tip (5-10 per cent) for good service. In cafés and bars, leave 15 per cent if you were served at a table (if the bill does not already include service) and 10-20c if standing at a counter or bar to drink.

At the theatre, opera or cinema, tip ushers 50c or more.

PLACES TO STAY
HOTELS

In this guide hotels have been classified by the official star system, reflecting level of comfort. In general for a double room you can expect to pay:

✩ - ✩✩ under €100
✩✩✩ - ✩✩✩✩ €100-300
✩✩✩✩✩✩ €300 plus

All of the hotels listed here have something special about them: beautiful surroundings, a distinctive atmosphere, and even the humblest are adequately comfortable. The local tourist offices will help you find accommodation on the spot; nevertheless you should try to book well in advance, especially if you're planning to travel between May and October. If you cancel the booking at least 72 hours in advance you can claim back part or all of your deposit. Hotels equipped to offer hospitality to the disabled are indicated in the tourist boards' hotel lists.

In all hotels the service charges are included in the rates. The total charge is exhibited on the back of the hotel room door. Breakfast is by law an optional extra charge. When booking a room, always specify if you want breakfast or not. Hotels are now obliged by law (for tax purposes) to issue an official receipt to customers: you should not leave the premises without this document.

THE CITY CENTRE

✩✩   **Villani**, Via delle Oche 11, *T* 055 239 6451, *F* 055 215 348, evillani@tin.it. Just 13 rooms, on the top floor with stunning views of the cathedral.

✩✩✩   **Della Signoria**, Via delle Terme 1, *T* 055 214 530, *F* 055 216 101, www.hoteldellasignoria.com. Charming traditional hotel situated in the heart of the historic centre.

Hermitage, Vicolo Marzio 1, *T* 055 287 216, *F* 055 212 208, www.hermitagehotel.com. An intimate and romantic hotel situated in the heart of old Florence, steps away from the Ponte Vecchio, Uffizi Gallery, Pitti Palace and Duomo; cosy atmosphere and beautiful rooftop garden.

Porta Rossa, Via Porta Rossa 19, *T* 055 287 551, *F* 055 282 179. A venerable establishment with 77 rooms and a panoramic suite in a medieval tower, in the heart of the old town.

Torre Guelfa, Borgo Santissimi Apostoli 8, *T* 055 239 6338, *F* 055 239 8577, www.florenceby.com/torreguelfa, torre:guelfa@ flashnet.it. A wonderful, small hotel in a 13c tower-house enjoying magnificent views over the city.

☆☆☆☆ **Berchielli**, Lungarno Acciaiuoli and Piazza del Limbo, *T* 055 264 061, *F* 055 218 636, www.berchielli.it. Seventy-six fully soundproofed and air-conditioned rooms in a beautifully renovated 14c palace.

Brunelleschi, Piazza Sant'Elisabetta 3, *T* 055 27370, *F* 055 219 653, www.hotelbrunelleschi.it. A pleasant place recently obtained by joining several very ancient buildings (including a 1000-year-old tower-house) mid-way between the Duomo and the Uffizi.

Continentale, Lungarno Acciaiuoli 2, *T* 055 272 622, *F* 055 283 139, www.lungarnohotels.com. Forty-three rooms and one magnificent penthouse suite situated on the right bank of the river Arno, just minutes away from the main museums and the most exclusive shopping district in Florence.

Gallery Hotel Art, Vicolo dell'Oro 5, *T* 055 27263, *F* 055 268 557, www.lungarnohotels.it. A high standard of comfort, just a block from the Ponte Vecchio; the view from the roof terrace is memorable.

☆☆☆☆☆ **Helvetia e Bristol**, Via de' Pescioni 2 (with restaurant), *T* 055 287 814, *F* 055 288 353, www.charminghotels.it. Refined elegance in an old hotel restored with the utmost care, opposite the Palazzo Strozzi.

Lungarno Suites, Lungarno Acciaiuoli 4, *T* 055 2726 8000, *F* 055 2726 8888, www.lungarnohotels.com. At the Ponte Vecchio, in the heart of Florence; suites offering tasteful modern décor and the service of a hotel.

Savoy, Piazza della Repubblica 7 (with restaurant), *T* 055 27351, *F* 055 273 5888, www.hotelsavoy.it. Elegant décor and the highest standards of accommodation, cuisine and personalized service in the historic Piazza della Repubblica, close to the Duomo and just steps away from the main museums, galleries and fashion houses.

OLTRARNO

☆ **Bandini**, Piazza Santo Spirito 9, *T* 055 215 308, *F* 055 282 761. Just 13 rooms, on the most fashionable square on Florence's left bank.

☆☆ **Boboli**, Via Romana 63, *T* 055 229 8645, *F* 055 233 7169, www.hotelboboli.com. Very simple and very convenient, in the heart of the Oltrarno; 18 rooms on three floors, with good views from those at the top.

La Scaletta, Via Guicciardini 13, *T* 055 283 028, *F* 055 289 562, www.venere.it/it/firenze/lascaletta. A few steps away from the Ponte Vecchio and the Palazzo Pitti, with magnificent panoramic terraces overlooking Florence and the surrounding hills.

✱✱✱ **Annalena**, Via Romana 32, *T* 055 229 600, *F* 055 222 403, www.hotelannalena.it. A pleasant, old-fashioned establishment in a former convent; some rooms have terraces or gardens.

Classic, Viale Machiavelli 25, *T* 055 229351, *F* 055 229 353, info@classichotel.it. Another lovely villa immersed in lush gardens just outside the Porta Romana.

David, Viale Michelangelo 1, *T* 055 681 1695, *F* 055 680 602, www.davidhotel.com. Boutique hotel in an 18c mansion not far from the Arno.

Silla, Via dei Renai 5 (with restaurant), *T* 055 234 2888, *F* 055 234 1437, www.hotelsilla.it. In a charming 16c palace on the left bank of the Arno.

✱✱✱✱ **Lungarno**, Borgo San Jacopo 14, *T* 055 27261, *F* 055 268 437, www.lungarnohotels.com. The flagship of the Lungarno Hotels (73 rooms, including 12 suites and one presidential suite), a recent refurbishment has enhanced the character that made it famous over the years; rooms and public spaces furnished with exquisite objects, antiques and original artworks by modern masters.

Torre di Bellosguardo, Via Roti Michelozzi 2 (with swimming pool), *T* 055 229 8145, *F* 055 229 008, torredibellosguardo@dada.it. A wonderful, eccentric castle situated on the hill of Bellosguardo and enjoying stunning views over Florence and the Arno valley; breakfast on the arcaded loggia and lunch by the pool in summer.

Villa Carlotta, Via Michele di Lando 3 (with restaurant), *T* 055 233 6134, *F* 055 233 6147, www.venere.it/it/firenze/villacarlotta. A lovely, comfortable villa, situated in the garden neighbourhood of Bobolino, just minutes from the Porta Romana and the Palazzo Pitti.

✱✱✱✱✱ **Grand Hotel**, Villa Cora Viale Miachiavelli 18 (with restaurant and swimming pool), *T* 055 229 8451, *F* 055 229 086, www.villa cora.com. In the most beautiful garden-quarter of Florence, a 48-room Neoclassical villa once the residence of Empress Eugenia, widow of Napoleon III.

SANTA MARIA NOVELLA

☆ **Scoti**, Via dei Tornabuoni 7, *T/F* 055 292 128,
hotelscoti@hotmail.com. Small (7 rooms) and friendly, in the
heart of the shopping district and a stone's throw away from
Piazza della Signoria and the Uffizi Gallery; old world charm,
breakfast in bed, but no bathrooms en suite.

☆☆ **Bretagna**, Lungarno Corsini 6, *T* 055 289 618, *F* 055 289 619,
www.bretagna.it. Located in the historic Palazzo Gianfigliazzi, in
the centre of Florence, on the right bank of the Arno within easy
walking distance of the major museums and points of interest.

☆☆☆ **Beacci Tornabuoni**, Via dei Tornabuoni 3 (with restaurant),
T 055 212 645, *F* 055 283 594, www.tornabuonihotels.com. A
hidden treasure, on the top floor, with rooftop terrace and good
views from most rooms.

☆☆☆☆ **Montebello Splendid**, Via Montebello 60, with restaurant,
T 055 239 8051, *F* 055 211 867, www.montebellosplendid.com. A
19c villa transformed into an intimate, comfortable hotel with a
particular attention to service; near the Teatro Comunale
(classical music, opera, ballet).

De la Ville, Piazza Antinori 1, *T* 055 238 1805, *F* 055 238 1809,
http://delaville.hotel-firenze.net/. A quietly luxurious
establishment located at the north end of the Via dei Tornabuoni,
in the midst of the best shops and the most significant
monuments.

Grand Hotel Minerva, Piazza Santa Maria Novella 16 (with
restaurant and swimming pool), *T* 055 27230, *F* 055 268 281,
www.sole.it. In a recently renovated historic building with good
views of Alberti's façade of Santa Maria Novella.

Kraft, Via Solferino 2 (with restaurant and rooftop swimming
pool), *T* 055 284 273, *F* 055 239 8267, www.krafthotel.it. A modern,
comfortable establishment near the Teatro Comunale, Florence's
leading venue for classical music, opera and ballet.

☆☆☆☆☆ **Grand Hotel**, Piazza Ognissanti 1 (with restaurant), *T* 055 288 781,
F 055 217 400, www.Starwood.com. A splendid former 18c palace
with richly appointed rooms, attentive service and historic
ambience.

Grand Hotel Villa Medici, Via il Prato 42 (with restaurant and
swimming pool), *T* 055 238 1331, *F* 055 238 1336,

www.Sinahotels.com. In an 18c palace, the only luxury hotel in the historic centre of Florence to offer a garden with a pool.

Westin Excelsior, Piazza Ognissanti 3 (with restaurant), **T** 055 27151, **F** 055 210 278, www.Starwood.com. Luxurious accommodation on the banks of the Arno, with spectacular views of the countryside and the rooftops and landmarks of Florence.

SAN MARCO

☆☆ **Casci**, Via Cavour 13, **T** 055 211 686, **F** 055 239 6461, www.hotelcasci.com. Small, friendly and centrally located, in a 15c palace that once belonged to composer Gioacchino Rossini.

☆☆☆ **Bencistà**, Via Benedetto da Maiano 4, Fiesole, **T/F** 055 59163, pensionebencista@iol.it. Charming family-run hotel romantically situated in the foothills between Florence and Fiesole, near where Leonardo conducted his experiments in flight.

Loggiato dei Serviti, Piazza Santissima Annunziata 3, **T** 055 289 592, **F** 055 289 595, www.loggiatodeiservitihotel.it. Built between 1517 and 1527 by the Servite Order to a design by the Antonio da Sangallo il Vecchio to match Brunelleschi's Foundling Hospital, across the square, the building was originally conceived to offer hospitality to prelates passing through the city of Florence; now meticulously restored and tastefully decorated.

Rapallo, Via Santa Caterina d'Alessandria 7 (with restaurant), **T** 055 472 412, **F** 055 470 385, www.venere.it/it/firenze/rapallo. A comfortable place just a few minutes' walk from the Piazza San Marco and from Santa Maria Novella station.

Royal, Via delle Ruote 52, **T** 055 330 342, **F** 055 490 976, www.florenceby.com/royalfirenze. A garden hotel in the old city centre just minutes from San Marco, Santa Maria Novella and the cathedral; some rooms have balconies.

☆☆☆☆ **Grand Hotel Baglioni**, Piazza Unità Italiana 6 (with restaurant), **T** 055 23580, **F** 055 235 88895, www.hotelbaglioni.it. In a 19c building, once the residence of the Carrega Bertolini princes, just 300m from Santa Maria Novella station and within easy walking distance of monuments, museums and shops; original beamed ceilings in many rooms and famous rooftop restaurant.

Sofitel, Via de'Cerretani 10 (with restaurant), **T** 055 238 1301, **F** 055 238 1312, www.florenceby.com/sofitelfirenze/. Eighty-four comfortable rooms in a renovated 18c palace, just a few steps

from the cathedral and around the corner from the Via dei
Tornabuoni shopping district.

✩✩✩✩✩ **Villa San Michele**, Via Doccia 4, Fiesole (with restaurant
and swimming pool), *T* 055 567 8200, *F* 055 567 8250,
www.orient- expresshotels.com. Surrounded by gardens
and woodland on the hill of Fiesole, a magnificent luxury hotel
enjoying superb views over Florence and the Arno valley.

SANTA CROCE

✩✩ **Chiazza**, Borgo Pinti 5, *T* 055 283 575, *F* 055 283 579,
www. venere.it/it/firenze/chiazza. Centrally located, with
comfortable rooms (all with bath en suite) overlooking a
bright, quiet courtyard.

✩✩✩✩ **J&J**, Via di Mezzo 20, *T* 055 26312, *F* 055 240 282,
www.jandj hotel.com. A former convent on an ancient street in the
heart of Florence: each room is different, all are furnished with
antiques and hand-woven fabrics; original frescoes, plasterwork
and a beautiful cloister with a well and Doric columns.

Mona Lisa, Borgo Pinti 27, *T* 055 247 9751, *F* 055 247 9755,
www.monnalisa.it. An attractive, unusual establishment in an
elegant Renaissance palace furnished with fine antique furniture,
old oil paintings and a number of art treasures, including the first
model for Giambologna's *Rape of the Sabines* and Neoclassical
drawings and statues by Giovanni Duprè (1817-82) the famous
sculptor from whom the owner's family is descended.

Ville sull'Arno, Lungarno Cristoforo Colombo 1 5 (with restaurant
and swimming pool), *T* 055 670 971, *F* 055 678 244,
www. villesullarno.it. A villa on the right bank of the Arno, once
the property of the family of Dante, and towards the end of the 19c
rented by the Macchiaioli painters, who turned it into a centre for
art studies where the Italian Impressionists and Post-
Impressionists could get together and exchange ideas; lovely
rooms and a shady garden especially precious in summer.

✩✩✩✩✩ **Regency**, Piazza d'Azeglio 3, with restaurant, *T* 055 245 247,
F 055 234 6735, www.regency-hotel.com. Peaceful, quiet and
luxurious, on a garden square only a few minutes' walk from the
main monuments and museums.

BED & BREAKFAST

B&B accommodation, usually in private homes, villas, etc, may be booked through a central agency.

Caffelletto, Via di Marciola 23, 50020 San Vincenzo a Torri (Firenze) Italy, *T* 055 7309145, *F* 055 768121, www.caffelletto.it

BedandBreakfast.com, 1855 Blake Street, Suite 201, Denver, CO 80202 USA, *T* 800 462 2632 (from outside the USA, 303 274 2800), *F* 303 274 2900, www. bedandbreakfast.com, support@bedandbreakfast.com

Bed & Breakfast in Europe, www.bedandbreakfastineurope.com/italia/en.htm.

The city of Florence

art glossary

Alberti, Leon Battista (1404–72) His personality, works, and breadth of learning make Alberti the prototype of the Renaissance 'universal man'. A distinguished Humanist scholar and a remarkable architect, he was the principal initiator of Renaissance art theory. Alberti's treatise *De Re Aedificatoria* (in English, *Ten Books on Architecture*), modelled on Vitruvius, written in the middle of the 15c and published in 1485, has been mandatory reading for architects ever since. His designs for the façades of Santa Maria Novella and the Palazzo Rucellai, in Florence, are among the highest achievements of Western architecture.

Ammannati, Bartolommeo (1511–92) The buildings of this sculptor and architect mark the transition from the classicizing Renaissance to the more exuberant Baroque style. Ammannati began his career as a sculptor, carving statues in various Italian cities in the 1530s and '40s. He was called to Rome in 1550 by Pope Julius III on the advice of the architect and art historian, Giorgio Vasari; but Cosimo de' Medici brought him back to Florence in 1555, and he spent most of his remaining career in service to the Medici. He finished the Biblioteca Laurenziana, begun by Michelangelo, and built the garden façade and courtyard of Palazzo Pitti; other major works by Ammannati in Florence are the Ponte Santa Trìnita (1567–69) and the Fountain of Neptune in the Piazza della Signoria.

Andrea del Sarto (1486–1530) Original name: Andrea d'Agnolo. The exquisitely composed and crafted works of this painter were instrumental in the development of painting in Florence and Rome in the first half of the 16c. His paintings may be seen in the Galleria degli Uffizi and the Galleria Palatina at Palazzo Pitti, in the Galleria dell'Accademia, at Santissima Annunziata and elsewhere around Florence; among his most famous works is the cycle of frescoes depicting the life of *St John the Baptist* in the Chiostro dello Scalzo.

Bandinelli, Baccio (1493?–1560) This Mannerist sculptor, strongly influenced by Michelangelo, was one of the principal artists at the court of Cosimo I de' Medici. He founded an academy for artists in the Vatican (1531) and one in Florence (c 1550). His copy of the *Laocoön* (Uffizi), and his statue of **Hercules and Cacus** (Piazza della Signoria) show an austere, rather arid sensibility that was highly valued at the Medici court.

Baroque art A style in the Western arts roughly coinciding with the 17c, though early manifestations in Italy occur in the late 16c. Baroque painting and sculpture are distinguished by the desire to evoke emotional states by appealing to the senses, often in dramatic ways. Some of the qualities most frequently associated with the Baroque are grandeur, sensuous richness, drama, vitality, movement, tension, emotional exuberance, and a tendency to blur distinctions between the various arts.

Bellini, Giovanni (1430-1516) The leading figure of the early Renaissance in Venice. Although the paintings for the hall of the Great Council in that city, considered his greatest works, were destroyed by fire in 1577, numerous other works (such as the *Sacred Allegory* in the Uffizi) show a steady evolution from purely religious, narrative emphasis to a new naturalism of setting and landscape.

Botticelli, Sandro (1445-1510) Original name: Alessandro di Mariano Filipepi. This superlative artist's two large paintings, the *Birth of Venus* and *Primavera*, displayed at the Uffizi, epitomize the spirit of the Renaissance for modern viewers. Botticelli's earlier compositions are imbued with Humanist literary and philosophical references, whereas his later works evince a deep sense of Christian piety.

Bronzino, Il (1503-72) Original name: Agnolo di Cosimo. The polished, elegant portraits of this Florentine painter are outstanding examples of the Mannerist style. They embody the courtly ideal under the Medici dukes (Bronzino was court painter to Cosimo I de' Medici from 1539 until his death), and they profoundly affected European court portraiture for the next century. His best-known work in Florence is the emotionally inexpressive, reserved, and noncommittal, yet arrestingly elegant and decorative portrait of *Eleonora di Toledo with Her Son Giovanni* in the Galleria degli Uffizi.

Brunelleschi, Filippo (1377-1446) An architect and engineer who was one of the pioneers of early Renaissance architecture in Italy, Brunelleschi is best known for the dome of the Florence cathedral, constructed with the aid of machines that he invented expressly for the project. He also designed several of the city's first Classical buildings: the Spedale degli Innocenti, the churches of San Lorenzo and Santo Spirito, the Sagrestia Vecchia at San Lorenzo, and the Cappella Pazzi at Santa Croce. A brilliant scholar as well as a 'practical' architect, Brunelleschi studied mathematics intensively and formulated the theory of linear perspective that was to become a basic element of Renaissance art. At the same time, he investigated ancient Roman architecture and acquired the knowledge of Classical form and ornament that he used as a foundation for his architecture. He was also receptive to the local Florentine tradition, which had flowered in the 11c and 12c in the Tuscan proto-Renaissance style found in churches such as San Miniato al Monte.

Caravaggio (1571?-1610) Byname of Michelangelo Merisi, the Lombard painter whose revolutionary technique of dramatic, selective illumination of form out of deep shadow, became a hallmark of Baroque painting. Scorning the traditional idealized interpretation of religious subjects, he took his models from the streets and painted them realistically. His *Sacrifice of Isaac* is one of his more dramatic works, and his *Medusa* and *Bacchus* are justly famous (all are in the Uffizi).

Castagno, Andrea del (1421-57) Pseudonym of Andrea di Bartolo, an influential painter known for the emotional power and naturalistic treatment of figures in his work. His *Last Supper* of about 1445, in the former convent of Sant'Apollonia in Florence, reveals the influence of Masaccio in the sculptural treatment of the figures, the concern with light, and the desire to create a credible and rational space. It also shows an acute interest in antiquity, evidenced by the use of fictive marble panels on the rear wall and of sphinxes for the bench ends, both of which are direct copies of Roman prototypes.

Cellini, Benvenuto (1500-71) Because of the lively account of himself and his period in his *Autobiography*, this sculptor and goldsmith has become one of the more picturesque figures of the Renaissance. His bronze statue of the youthful *Perseus* holding aloft the head of Medusa, in the Loggia della Signoria, is a magnificent expression of Florentine Mannerism that reveals the artist's profound understanding of cast sculpture: void is almost as important as solid in this light, airy composition, which would have been impossible to make in marble.

Chiaroscuro Distribution of light and shade, apart from colour in a painting.

Cimabue (before 1251-1302) His great contemporary, Dante, recognized the importance of Cimabue and placed him at the forefront of Italian painters, and scholars from the 14c to the present have recognized his art and career as the dividing line between the old and the new traditions in Western European painting. The earliest biography of Cimabue, by Vasari, states that he was born in 1240 and died in 1300. The dates can only be approximations, for it is documented that Cimabue was alive and working in Pisa in 1302. Cimabue's character may be reflected in his name, which can best be translated as 'bullheaded'.

Classicism and Neoclassicism Historical tradition or aesthetic attitudes based on the art of ancient Greece and Rome in antiquity. Classicism refers either to the art produced in antiquity or to later art inspired by that of antiquity; Neoclassicism always refers to the art produced later but inspired by antiquity. The Classical tradition did not die out during the Middle Ages, but because of the efforts of 15c and 16c Italians to absorb the Classicism of antiquity, the Italian Renaissance was the first period of thoroughgoing Classicism after antiquity. The architect Leon Battista Alberti equated Classicism and beauty and defined beauty in architecture as 'the harmony and concord of all the parts achieved by following well-founded rules [based on the study of ancient works] and resulting in a unity such that nothing could be added or taken away or altered except for the worse'. He said that the 'sculptor should endeavour as much as possible to express by both the deportment ... and bearing ... of the figure, the life and character ... of the person'. In painting, artists were to choose subjects that glorified man, use figures suited to the actions being represented, and imitate the appearance of actions in the natural world.

Della Robbia family Luca della Robbia (in full, Luca di Simone di Marco della Robbia, 1399/1400-82) was the founder of a family studio primarily associated with the production of works in enamelled terracotta. The earliest documented work executed wholly in that medium is a lunette of the *Resurrection* over the door of the northern sacristy of the cathedral (1442-5). Andrea della Robbia (in full, Andrea di Marco di Simone della Robbia, 1435-1525) was Luca's nephew and assumed control of the family workshop after his uncle's death. Giovanni della Robbia (1469-1529) was Andrea's son and Luca's great-nephew, who took over the family workshop after the death of his father.

Desiderio da Settignano (c 1430-64) The portrait busts and marble low reliefs for which this sculptor has become famous are unrivalled for subtlety and technical accomplishment. Desiderio's delicate, sensitive, highly original style is exquisitely expressed in his sensuous portrait busts of a *Young Woman* and *Boy* in the Bargello, and his tomb sculptures in Santa Croce.

Domenico Veneziano (active by 1438-died in 1461) Byname of Domenico di Bartolomeo da Venezia. This early Italian Renaissance artist was one of the founders of the 15c Florentine school of painting. He was first trained in the International Gothic manner in Venice, where it is likely he saw paintings by northern European artists; he settled in Florence about 1439 and, except for brief periods, worked there until his death. Only two signed works by Domenico survive: the Uffizi *Santa Lucia dei Magnoli Altarpiece*, dated 1445, and a much-damaged fresco of the *Virgin and Child Enthroned* from the Carnesecchi Tabernacle (National Gallery, London).

Donatello (1386-1466) Full name: Donato de' Bardi. The greatest of all early Renaissance sculptors. He had a more detailed and wide-ranging knowledge of ancient sculpture than any other artist of his day, and his work was inspired by ancient visual examples, which he often daringly transformed. Though he was traditionally viewed as essentially a realist, he was in fact much more.

Duccio di Buoninsegna (1260-1319) One of the great Italian painters of the Middle Ages and the founder of the Sienese school of painting, Duccio fused the new spirituality of the Gothic style with the static formality of the Byzantine tradition, strengthened by a clear understanding of its evolution from Classical roots. The Uffizi *Maestà* is one of his more famous works.

Fra' Angelico (1400-55) Original name: Guido di Pietro; also called Fra' Giovanni da Fiesole. One of the greater early Florentine Renaissance painters, whose works embody a composed religious attitude and reflect a strong Classical influence. Most of his early work consists of frescoes that he painted for the Monastery of San Marco in Florence while he was in residence there.

Fra' Bartolomeo (1472-1517) Full name: Bartolomeo di Paoli del Fattorino; also called Baccio della Porta. A prominent exponent of the High Renaissance style in early 16c Florence, this painter took the Dominican habit in 1500 and, in 1504, established a studio at the monastery of San Marco.

Gaddi, Taddeo (c 1300-66?) Taddeo Gaddi was Giotto's most faithful pupil and, after his master's death, the leading Florentine painter for three decades.

Ghiberti, Lorenzo (1378-1455) An important early Italian Renaissance sculptor whose baptistery doors (*Gates of Paradise*) are considered one of the great masterpieces of Italian art. Other works include three bronze statues for Orsanmichele and a number of treatises on art history and theory.

Giambologna (1529-1608) Full name: Jean Boulogne or Giovanni Bologna. A Flemish sculptor who went to Rome around 1555, where he discovered Hellenistic sculpture and the works of Michelangelo. Settling in Florence in 1557, he came into the circle of Francesco de' Medici, for whom many of his more important works were made. His ability to capture fleeting expression, and the vivacity and sensual delight of his mature style, anticipate the Baroque sculpture of Gianlorenzo Bernini.

Giorgione (c 1477-1510) Also called Giorgio da Castelfranco; original name Giorgio Barbarelli. This extremely influential Venetian painter was one of the initiators of a High Renaissance style. His most famous work is *The Tempest* (c 1505) in the Galleria dell'Accademia in Venice; but the same qualities of mood and mystery pervade the two small panels by Giorgione and his pupils in the Uffizi, *Moses Undergoing Trial by Fire* (c 1502-5) and *The Judgement of Solomon* (c 1502-8), as well as the *Three Ages of Man* (c 1500) in the Galleria Palatina at Palazzo Pitti.

Giotto (1266/7 or 1276-1337) Giotto di Bondone is the most important Italian painter of the 14c. He is believed to have been a pupil of the Florentine painter Cimabue and to have decorated chapels in Assisi, Rome, Padua, Florence, and Naples with frescoes and panel paintings in tempera. Because little of his life and few of his works are documented, however, attributions and a stylistic chronology of his paintings remain problematic and often highly speculative. Giotto developed a new pictorial style that relies on clear, simple structure and great psychological penetration rather than on the flat, linear decorativeness and hierarchical compositions of his predecessors and contemporaries; in this sense he is a precursor of the Renaissance painters who emerged more than a century later.

Ghirlandaio, Domenico (1449-94) Original name: Domenico di Tommaso Bigordi. An early Renaissance painter noted for his detailed narrative frescoes, which include portraits of leading citizens in contemporary dress, Domenico was the son of a goldsmith and his nickname 'Ghirlandaio' was derived from his father's skill in making garlands.

Gothic art A style of painting, sculpture and architecture that flourished in Europe during the Middle Ages. Gothic art evolved from Romanesque art and lasted roughly from the 13c to the 15c in Florence. Architecture was the most important and original art form during the Gothic period. The principal structural elements of Gothic architecture are ribbed vaults and pointed (ogival or lancet) arches, which distribute thrust from heavy walls and ceilings in a highly efficient manner. These elements enabled Gothic masons to build much larger and taller buildings than their Romanesque predecessors and to give their structures more complicated ground plans.

The term Gothic was coined by Italian Renaissance writers who attributed the invention (and what to them was the non-Classical ugliness) of medieval architecture to the barbarian Gothic tribes that had destroyed the Roman Empire and its Classical culture. The term retained its derogatory overtones until the 19c.

Humanism Although the spirit of the Renaissance ultimately took many forms, it was expressed earliest by the intellectual movement called Humanism. Humanism was initiated by secular men of letters rather than by the scholar-clerics who had dominated medieval intellectual life. Humanism began in Italy. Its predecessors were people like Dante and Petrarch, and its chief protagonists included the Florentines Marsilio Ficino and Pico della Mirandola.

Humanism had several significant features. First, it took human nature in all of its various manifestations and achievements as its subject. Second, it stressed the unity and compatibility of the truth found in all philosophical and theological schools and systems, a doctrine known as syncretism. Third, it emphasized the dignity of man. In place of the medieval ideal of a life of penance as the highest and noblest form of human activity, the Humanists looked to the struggle of creation and the attempt to exert mastery over nature. Finally, Humanism looked forward to a rebirth of a lost human spirit and wisdom. In the course of striving to recover these lost values, however, the Humanists sparked a new spiritual and intellectual outlook and cultivated a new body of knowledge.

Leonardo da Vinci (1452-1519) Painter, draftsman, sculptor, architect, and engineer, Leonardo, perhaps more than any other figure, epitomized the Renaissance Humanist ideal. The fame that Leonardo enjoyed in his lifetime and that, filtered by historical criticism, has remained undimmed to the present day rests largely on his unlimited desire for knowledge, which guided all his thinking and behaviour.

Lippi, Fra Filippo (1406-69) Florentine painter in the second generation of Renaissance artists. While exhibiting the strong influence of Masaccio (eg in *Madonna and Child*, 1437) and Fra Angelico (eg, in *Coronation of the Virgin*, c 1445), his work achieves a distinctive clarity of expression. Legend and tradition surround his unconventional life.

Mannerist art The style and practice that predominated in Italy from the end of the High Renaissance in the 1520s to the beginnings of the Baroque age around 1590. Mannerism originated as a reaction to the harmonious Classicism and the idealized naturalism of High Renaissance art as practised by Leonardo, Michelangelo and Raphael. An obsession with style and technique in figural composition often outweighed the importance of subject matter. The highest value was placed upon the apparently effortless solution of intricate artistic problems, such as the portrayal of the nude in complex and artificial poses.

Mantegna, Andrea (1431?–1506) A painter and engraver, the first fully Renaissance artist of northern Italy.

Masaccio (1401–28) Byname of Tommaso di Giovanni di Simone Guidi, important Florentine painter of the early Renaissance whose frescoes in the Brancacci Chapel of the Church of Santa Maria del Carmine in Florence (c 1427) remained influential throughout the Renaissance. In the span of only six years, Masaccio radically transformed Florentine painting. The intellectuality of his conceptions, the monumentality of his compositions, and the high degree of naturalism in his works mark Masaccio as a pivotal figure in Renaissance painting.

Masolino (1383–1440/7) Nickname of Tommaso di Cristoforo Fini, a painter who developed a lyrical style representing a compromise between the International Gothic manner and the early Renaissance art of Florence.

Medici The banking family that ruled Florence and, later, Tuscany, during the period from 1434 to 1737, except for two brief intervals (from 1494–1512 and 1527–30). Their passion for the arts and letters was a major driving force of the Italian Renaissance. Cosimo il Vecchio (1389–1464), Lorenzo il Magnifico (1449–92) and Cosimo I (1519–74), especially, were brilliant, enlightened patrons.

Michelangelo (1475–1564) In full, Michelangelo di Lodovico Buonarroti Simoni. The Italian Renaissance sculptor, painter, architect, and poet who exerted an unequalled influence on the development of Western art. Michelangelo was considered the greatest living artist in his lifetime, and ever since then he has been held to be one of the more important artists of all time. A number of his works in painting, sculpture, and architecture rank among the most famous in existence. Although the frescoes on the ceiling of the Sistine Chapel are probably the best known of his works today, the artist thought of himself primarily as a sculptor.

Michelozzo (1396-1472) In full, Michelozzo di Bartolommeo. Closely associated with his principal patrons, the Medici, this Florentine architect and sculptor followed Cosimo de' Medici into exile to Venice in 1433. Upon Cosimo's triumphant return to power in Florence in 1434, Michelozzo's architectural career began in earnest with several important commissions. In 1436 he began the complete rebuilding of the ruined monastery of San Marco; in 1444–5 he directed the similar reconstruction of the large complex of church buildings at Santissima Annunziata; he temporarily succeeded Filippo Brunelleschi as architect for the cathedral of Florence upon the latter's death in 1446; and he designed Cosimo de' Medici's Florentine mansion (1444–59).

Orcagna, Andrea (c 1308-c 1368) Original name, Andrea di Cione. The most prominent Florentine painter, sculptor, and architect of the mid-14c, Orcagna was also the leading member of a family of painters that included three younger brothers: Nardo, Matteo, and Jacopo (died after 1398) di Cione.

Parmigianino (1503-40) Byname of Girolamo Francesco Maria Mazzola or Mazzuoli. This painter from Parma was one of the first artists to develop an elegant, sophisticated Mannerist style that became a formative influence on the post-High Renaissance generation.

Perugino (c 1450-1523) Byname of Pietro di Cristoforo Vannucci. This early Renaissance painter of the Umbrian school was the teacher of Raphael; his work anticipated High Renaissance ideals in its compositional clarity, sense of spaciousness, and economy of formal elements.

Piero della Francesca (1420-92) A painter whose serene, disciplined exploration of perspective had little influence on his contemporaries but came to be recognized in the 20c as a major contribution to the Italian Renaissance. Piero received his early training in Florence but spent the active part of his career in Urbino, Arezzo, Rimini, and his native Borgo San Sepolcro, in Umbria.

Pollaiolo, Antonio del (1432/33-98) and Piero del (1443-96) Original names Antonio e Piero di Jacopo d'Antonio Benci. These brothers produced numerous paintings, sculptures, engravings and gold objects under a combined signature. The Pollaiolo brothers had significant influence on the development of Florentine art, and maintained one of the more important workshops in Florence during the late 15c.

Pontormo, Jacopo da (1494-1557) Original name Jacopo Carrucci. This innovative Florentine painter, who Vasari says studied with Leonardo da Vinci and Andrea del Sarto, broke away from High Renaissance Classicism to create a more personal, expressive style sometimes classified as early Mannerism.

Raphael (1483-1520) In Italian, Raffaello Sanzio. This master painter and architect of the Italian High Renaissance is best known for his Madonnas (several of which are in the Galleria Palatina at Palazzo Pitti) and for his large figure compositions in the Vatican in Rome. His work is admired for its clarity of form and ease of composition and for its visual achievement of the Humanist ideal of human grandeur.

Renaissance art Literally 'rebirth', the term Renaissance refers to the period in European civilization immediately following the Middle Ages, conventionally held to have been characterized by a surge of interest in Classical learning and values. The Renaissance originated in Florence in the early 15c and thence spread throughout Italy and Europe, gradually replacing the Gothic style of the late Middle Ages. It encouraged a revival of naturalism in painting and sculpture, and of Classical forms and ornament in architecture

Romanesque art The name Romanesque refers to the fusion of Roman, Carolingian and Ottonian, Byzantine and Germanic traditions that characterized European art from around 1000 to about 1150. Although perhaps the most striking advances in Romanesque art were made in France, the style was current in all parts of Europe except those eastern areas that preserved a fully-fledged Byzantine tradition. Its geographic distribution resulted in a wide variety of local types.

Rossellino, Antonio (1427-79) A prolific Italian Renaissance sculptor who was the youngest brother of the architect and sculptor Bernardo Rossellino. His greatest work is the **Tomb of the Cardinal of Portugal** in San Miniato al Monte, an elaborate and decorative combination of architectural and sculptural elements.

Rossellino, Bernardo (1409-64) An influential early Italian Renaissance architect and sculptor trained by Filippo Brunelleschi and influenced by Luca della Robbia and Lorenzo Ghiberti. His style exhibited a moderate Classicism. His masterpiece, the **Tomb of Leonardo Bruni** in Santa Croce, ranks with the greatest achievements of early Renaissance sculpture.

Rosso Fiorentino (1495-1540) Full name, Giovanni Battista di Jacopo Rosso. This early Mannerist painter received his training in the studio of Andrea del Sarto, alongside his contemporary, Pontormo. The first works of the two young painters combined influences from Michelangelo and from northern Gothic engravings in a novel style, which departed from the tenets of High Renaissance art and was characterized by an emphasis on emotion.

Sangallo family In this outstanding family of Florentine Renaissance architects the most prominent members were Antonio da Sangallo the Elder (1455-1535); his older brother Giuliano da Sangallo (1445?-1516); Antonio (Giamberti) da Sangallo the Younger (1483-1546), the nephew of Giuliano and Antonio Sangallo the Elder; and Francesco da Sangallo (1494-1576), the son of Giuliano.

Tintoretto (c 1518-94) Byname of Jacopo Robusti. A great Mannerist painter of the Venetian school and one of the more important artists of the late Renaissance. He is represented in Florence by two paintings, **Leda and the Swan** in the Uffizi, and the quietly impressive portrait of **Alvise Cornaro** in the Galleria Palatina.

Titian (1488/90-1576) In Italian, Tiziano Vecellio. The greatest Renaissance painter of the Venetian school was recognized early in his own lifetime as an extraordinary painter, and his reputation has never suffered a decline. Titian's **Venus of Urbino**, in the Uffizi, may be his single most influential work; four other important paintings are in the Galleria Palatina at Palazzo Pitti.

Uccello, Paolo (1397-1475) His original name was Paolo di Dono. A Florentine painter whose work attempted uniquely to reconcile two distinct artistic styles - the essentially decorative late Gothic and the new heroic style of the early Renaissance. Probably his most famous paintings are three panels representing *The Battle of San Romano* (c 1456), one of which is in the Uffizi. His careful and sophisticated perspective studies are clearly evident in *The Flood* (1447-8) in Santa Maria Novella.

Vasari, Giorgio (1511-74) Italian painter, architect, and writer who is best known for his important biographies of Italian Renaissance artists *Le Vite de' più eccellenti architetti, pittori, et scultori italiani* (1550 and 1568; in English *Lives of the Most Eminent Painters, Sculptors, and Architects*).

Verrocchio, Andrea del (1435-88) Florentine sculptor and painter and the teacher of Leonardo da Vinci. His bronze *David* in the Bargello and *Winged Putto* in Palazzo Vecchio are justly famous.

Zuccari, Federico (1540-1609) This painter and art theorist became the central figure of the Roman Mannerist school and, after the death of Titian, possibly the best known painter in Europe. In 1565 Federico worked in Florence under Giorgio Vasari and codified the theory of Mannerism in *L'idea de' scultori, pittori e architetti* (*The Idea of Sculptors, Painters, and Architects*, 1607) and in a series of frescoes in his own house in Rome (Palazzo Zuccari). In 1593 he became the first president of the Academy of St Luke in Rome. In England, in 1575, Zuccari painted portraits of Queen Elizabeth I and the Earl of Leicester. Later commissions included the painting of the dome of Florence Cathedral (1575–9).

First edition 2004

Published by A&C Black Publishers Ltd
37 Soho Square, London W1D 3QZ

ISBN 0-7136-6836-9

Published in the United States of America by
WW Norton & Company, Inc
500 Fifth Avenue, New York, NY 10110, USA

ISBN 0-393-32592-X

Published in Canada by Penguin Books Canada Limited
10 Alcorn Avenue, Toronto, Ontario M4V 3BE

Series devised by Gemma Davies
Series designed by Jocelyn Lucas
Editorial and production: Gemma Davies, Jocelyn Lucas, Lilla Nwenu-Msimang, Miranda Robson, Kim Teo, Judy Tither

Maps by Mapping Company Ltd

Front cover photograph and inside cover: *Birth of Venus* (detail) by Botticelli, Galleria degli Uffizi, Florence © Photo SCALA, Florence - courtesy of the Ministero Beni e Att. Culturali
Back cover photograph: © Jocelyn Lucas
Photographs inside the book: all photographs by Paul Blanchard with the exception of p 34, the *Doni Tondo* by Michelangelo, Galleria degli Uffizi, Florence © Photo SCALA, Florence - courtesy of the Ministero Beni e Att. Culturali, and p 100, the *Deposition* (detail) by Fra' Angelico, Museo de San Marco, Florence © Photo SCALA, Florence - courtesy of the Ministero Beni e Att. Culturali

Author's acknowledgements. The author wishes to thank his family, for their unending patience; art historian Susan Haywood for her thoughtful revision of the manuscript.

Printed and bound in Singapore by Tien Wah Press (Pte.) Ltd

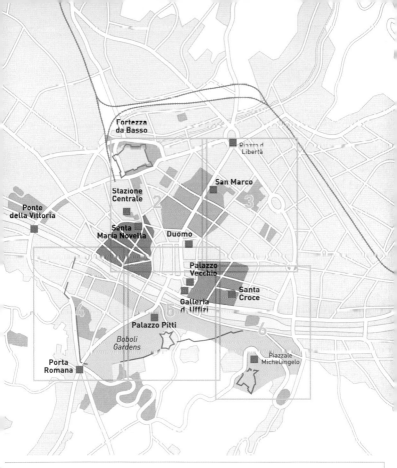

Fortezza
da Basso

Piazza d
Libertà

San Marco

Stazione
Centrale

Ponte
della Vittoria

Santa
Maria Novella

Duomo

Palazzo
Vecchio

Santa
Croce

Galleria
d. Uffizi

Palazzo Pitti

*Boboli
Gardens*

Piazzale
Michelangelo

Porta
Romana

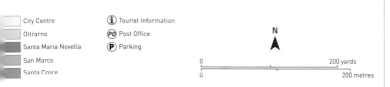

KEY MAP TO ATLAS SECTION

City Centre

Oltrarno

Santa Maria Novella

San Marco

Santa Croce

ⓘ Tourist Information

🅟🅾 Post Office

🅟 Parking

N

0		200 yards
0		200 metres

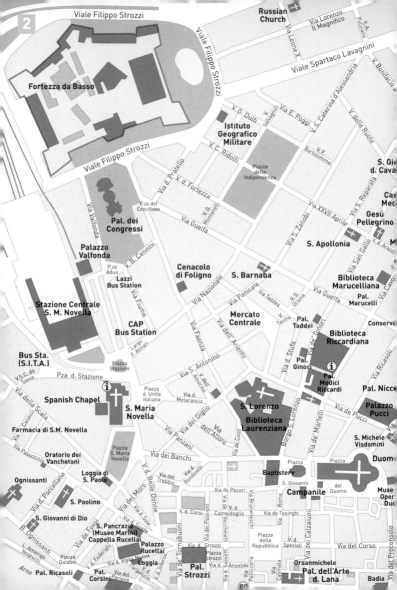

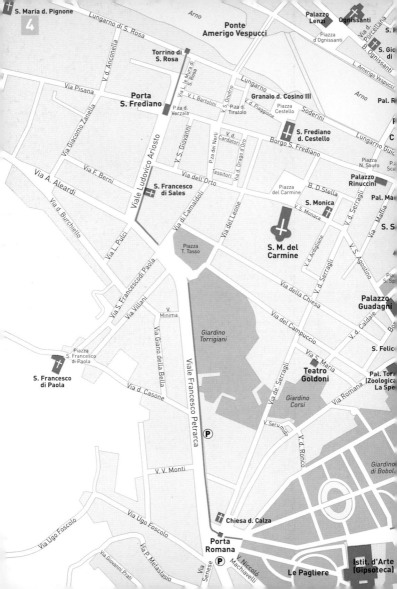

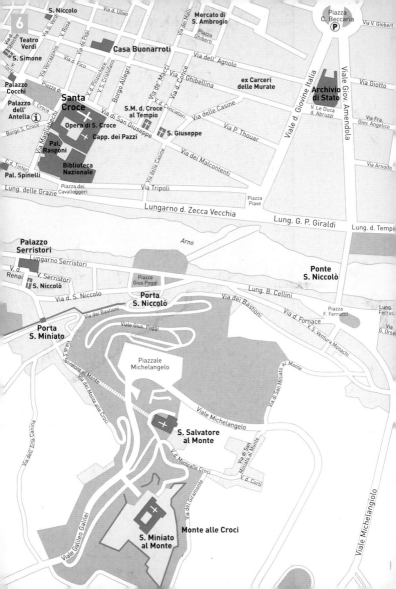